"Excellent! Timeless wisdom is dispensed with clarity and refreshing lightness. If you are serious about raising great kids, you must read this book."

—MEG MEEKER, MD, pediatrician and author of the best-selling
Strong Fathers, Strong Daughters

"*Secure Daughters, Confident Sons* provides a powerful vision of raising girls and boys in an ever-changing world. Combining brain science with a Christian perspective, Glenn Stanton inspires parents and teachers to be at once visionary and practical. This book is inspiring and far reaching."

—MICHAEL GURIAN, author of *The Wonder of Boys* and
The Wonder of Girls

"In this delightful book, Glenn Stanton lovingly reveals the secrets of raising healthy sons and daughters."

—LOUANN BRIZENDINE, MD, author of *The Female Brain*
and *The Male Brain*

"*Secure Daughters, Confident Sons* will help you become a secure, confident parent in raising gender-healthy children. It offers rich insight and highly practical applications for empowering your children to be all God intended when He made them male or female."

—ROBERT LEWIS, founder of Men's Fraternity and author
of *Raising a Modern-Day Knight*

"The culture tells us that the lines separating male and female are meaningless, but Glenn Stanton has tapped into the critical importance of recognizing and cultivating the distinct qualities of boys and girls. His book gives parents practical tools to help them appreciate and develop the femininity of their daughters and the masculinity of their sons. Glenn's work demonstrates that each gender is uniquely gifted by God for a purpose, and by celebrating these gender-specific behaviors and attitudes, we strengthen families and help men and women find purpose and fulfillment."

—JIM DALY, president and CEO of Focus on the Family

"Every parent is raising a boy or girl into manhood or womanhood. There is no third option. Glenn Stanton has done parents and grandparents a noble service in helping us understand—based on insights of emerging science and the ancient wisdom of Christianity—how mothers and fathers both guide their children into healthy, balanced, and authentic masculinity and femininity. I know moms and dads—as well as those who want to understand how and why gender matters—will be helped by this important book."

—JOHN ROSEMOND, family psychologist and author of
The Well-Behaved Child: Discipline That Really Works!

"Glenn Stanton has courageously addressed one of the most challenging yet rarely discussed aspects of parenting: what is the essence of your child's gender? His observations are not only insightful, but also practical. In a world steeped in gender confusion, this resource is invaluable."

—DR. JULI SLATTERY, author and psychologist, Focus on the Family

"We live in a time of almost breathtaking confusion over things that should be basic, like the difference between boys and girls. Parents need good guidance in the midst of such confusion, and Glenn Stanton offers this kind of advice in *Secure Daughters, Confident Sons*. The secular world tells us that masculinity and femininity are merely social constructs that we must learn to leave behind, but Stanton believes that a proper understanding of manhood and womanhood is essential to Christian faithfulness and human happiness. I am thankful for his conviction and his courage."

—DR. R. ALBERT MOHLER JR., president of the Southern Baptist
Theological Seminary

Secure Daughters,
Confident Sons

Secure Daughters, Confident Sons

How Parents GUIDE THEIR CHILDREN *into*
AUTHENTIC MASCULINITY *and* FEMININITY

Glenn T. Stanton

MULTNOMAH
BOOKS

SECURE DAUGHTERS, CONFIDENT SONS
PUBLISHED BY MULTNOMAH BOOKS
12265 Oracle Boulevard, Suite 200
Colorado Springs, Colorado 80921

All Scripture quotations, unless otherwise indicated, are taken from the New King James Version®. Copyright © 1982 by Thomas Nelson Inc. Used by permission. All rights reserved. Scripture quotations marked (MSG) are taken from The Message by Eugene H. Peterson. Copyright © 1993, 1994, 1995, 1996, 2000, 2001, 2002. Used by permission of NavPress Publishing Group. All rights reserved. Scripture quotations marked (NIV) are taken from the Holy Bible, New International Version®. NIV®. Copyright © 1973, 1978, 1984 by Biblica Inc.™ Used by permission of Zondervan. All rights reserved worldwide. www.zondervan.com.

Details in some anecdotes and stories have been changed to protect the identities of the persons involved.

ISBN 978-1- 60142-294-1
ISBN 978-1- 60142-295-8 (electronic)

Cover design by Kristopher Orr; cover image by David Trood, Getty Images

Published in the United States by WaterBrook Multnomah, an imprint of the Crown Publishing Group, a division of Random House Inc., New York.

MULTNOMAH and its mountain colophon are registered trademarks of Random House Inc.

Library of Congress Cataloging-in-Publication Data
Stanton, Glenn T., 1962–
    Secure daughters, confident sons : how parents guide their children into authentic masculinity and femininity / Glenn T. Stanton. — 1st ed.
        p. cm.
    Includes bibliographical references (p.   ).
    ISBN 978-1-60142-294-1 — ISBN 978-1-60142-295-8 (electronic)
    1. Child rearing—Religious aspects—Christianity. 2. Sex role—Religious aspects—
Christianity. 3. Sex role in children. I. Title.
    BV4529.S797 2011
    248.8′45—dc22

                                                    2010041763

Printed in the United States of America
2011—First Edition

10 9 8 7 6 5 4 3 2 1

SPECIAL SALES
Most WaterBrook Multnomah books are available at special quantity discounts when purchased in bulk by corporations, organizations, and special-interest groups. Custom imprinting or excerpting can also be done to fit special needs. For information, please e-mail SpecialMarkets@WaterBrookMultnomah.com or call 1-800-603-7051.

Affectionately dedicated to five amazing gifts:

Olivia Glenn
Reed Schaeffer
Sophia Grace
Tess Elizabeth
Isabel Lee

You each have taught me profoundly about the beauty,
mystery, and wonder of humanity
found in what it means to be male and female
without even being aware of it.

One of the greatest joys of my life has been watching you grow
and become God's women and man.

CONTENTS

ACKNOWLEDGMENTS

Some authors write books to fulfill a contract. Others write books because they feel a particular volume just has to be written and they cannot rest until it is completed. My reason for writing this book falls into the latter category. It addresses a vital issue of our age.

Three folks had a very direct role in the formation of this book. First is my literary agent, Blythe Daniel, who helped me find a good publisher to work with. She helped usher the book through from early idea stage to final product. And to make the whole feat a bit more interesting, she had twins while caring for her sweet toddler in the midst of it all. That's awesome, folks. Laura Barker, the gifted editorial director at WaterBrook Multnomah, maintained a smart vision for the project from the start and helped with wise and patient guidance. Brad Lewis, whom I had the fortune of working on each of my other books with, was a masterful final editor who made my words, ideas, and research sound better than they originally were. I was blessed to have this mighty team of three to work so closely with.

My wife, Jackie, and four of my kids gave me up for long hours to read countless journal articles and books on the subjects covered in these pages, as well as the extensive process of writing, editing, and rewriting. I did a great deal of this work during my oldest daughter's drama practices as I waited around, hunched over journal articles, books, and laptop, in the quiet recesses of her school's hallways while she was practicing with her cast in *Annie Get Your Gun.* A husband and father of five with a full-time job and travel schedule must multitask deftly.

Many folks kept me company via iPod during the research and writing hours: David Byrne, Jenny Lewis, The Kinks, Leonard Cohen, Patti Smith, Tom Waits, Art Blakey and the Jazz Messengers, Nico, Warren Zevon, Patty Griffin, Mulatu Astatke, Elvis Costello, and Mark Mothersbaugh, to name the most inspirational.

I hope that you, the reader, feel as I do, that this is a book that needed to be written. I pray it guides you in the vital and necessary task of raising boys and girls to be great men and women.

The Importance of Difference

Scott is all boy. At age six, he's the apple of his dad's eye. He learned quickly how to catch a football, kick a soccer ball, and swing a bat. Dad is itching to help him become a pro. The little bruiser loves to be with dad and soaks up every drop of his attention. But he also seems to have a great interest in caring for small animals, nurturing them as if he were their mom. When he and dad are playing in the front yard and a dog comes by, little Scott forgets all about the game and runs straight for the animal. This concerns dad...and mom too, but for different reasons. Dad wonders what normal boy allows anything to distract him from playing ball, other than perhaps a pretty girl. But certainly not this uncontrollable attraction to hugging dogs. Why can't his boy be a little more *boy*? Shouldn't he be caring more about "big boy" things by now? Has mom's concern for his safety—what if the dog bites?—encouraged Scott to be a little too soft? Should dad get him a dog—or take him hunting instead?

Alisa is a princess. Not specifically one princess, but several in any given day. Sometimes she's Cinderella, sometimes Snow White, other times Jasmine or Ariel. Most often, she's any kind of princess she can cobble together out of her available dress-up resources and from the creativity of her imagination. For Alisa, the frillier and shinier the better. Her mom is uncomfortable with Alisa being so stereotypical. She doesn't like the unrealistic role models of the Disneybots so prevalent among girls today. But what should Alisa's mom do? She always intended for her daughter to be a strong and independent woman, and this road lined with glitter and satin isn't the one she feels will ultimately take Alisa there.

Every one of us spends every day being either a man or a woman. But what does that really mean? What do male qualities really look like? What are essentially female characteristics? Do these qualities even exist? How do we *be* male or female—and how do we know when we aren't?

At its core, this book is simply about what everyone is. And that's either male or female. For all the diversity we see in the world, the different sorts of human beings who have populated our world throughout history have been made up of only two major kinds. And all the infinite human variety around us stems from these essential two types. There are a zillion and three ways to be a healthy, well-rounded man or woman. But at the same time, there are behaviors, attitudes, and perspectives that we universally and specifically understand as masculine or feminine. Unmistakably.

That brings us to the primary purpose of this book.

With human sex differences, most often the discussion these days unfortunately runs to one extreme or the other. In one corner, we have the "nothing to see here" folks who believe that sex differences are minor, biological "plumbing" issues and that gender is a concept created largely by cultural assumptions, prejudices, and sexism intended to keep people in their places.[1]

In the other corner, we have the vigorous Macho Joes and the Pretty-in-Pinks. Pure and simple, neat and easy: a boy is wild, only interested in contact sports, hunting, and getting dirty. A girl is only a girl if she is captivated by makeup, clothes, babies, gentleness, and sweetness. They would have us believe that any boy or girl who doesn't fit neatly into one of these two boxes isn't healthy or well adjusted.

Is there any territory between these two extremes? a space where we can talk truly and universally about male and female differences? I know there is, and it's why I wrote this book. As parents raising little people whom nature signed up to represent one of these two types, shouldn't we be more interested in helping them navigate the vast terrain in the middle than shoving them into either of the corners?

This is the space we'll be exploring together to gain a clearer understanding of what's truly and authentically male or female and how this translates into parenting children who are distinctly unique from us, in partnership with a spouse whose essential makeup is fundamentally different from our own. I believe this task—raising daughters secure in their femininity and sons confident in their masculinity—is an important one for parents, and it just so happens that the natural and social sciences agree. This is the first book that addresses this important topic altogether, much less in this depth, drawing from the breadth of established and emerging scientific discovery and examining this research in the light of the Christian story. We explore this question by asking not just what masculinity or femininity looks like in your nation or part of the world but across human experience, because this is where we understand it best and most authentically.

If each of us is male or female, then every day of our lives and every interaction is colored, indeed *determined*, by this first fundamental difference. No person is exempt or ever will be. And it has been this way since the first two humans arrived on the scene.

The two underlying questions we need to explore that stem from this fact are these:

1. How do we develop from childhood to healthy adulthood along one of these two lines?
2. What role does the gender or sex of parents play in guiding children in this process?

Our singular goal is nothing other than a healthy family of well-adjusted, happy human beings, because to be human is to be gendered.

So let's start at square one.

ARE THERE REALLY ESSENTIAL GENDER DIFFERENCES?

Maybe your interest in this subject goes back to your own childhood. How did you develop? Your kids have a vested interest in this question. Before we get into this fascinating discovery, let me invite you to pause for a moment to think about your own gender and its virtue. No deep or heavy stuff. Just sit back, clear your mind, and think with me for a moment.

For all of our differences and our unique stories about growing up in different places of the world—perhaps in strange and wonderful families—maturing into adults, we all started the same way: in the dark, warm security of our mother's womb. I know this about you.

You grew day by day with all the potential and promise you'd eventually realize. Within weeks, the news of your existence changed a number of people's lives forever in important ways. Great *consequence* and *significance* came from your existence. Your mother's first two thoughts of you were likely this, and in this order, probably not too far apart:

I'm pregnant!

Wow, I wonder what it is?

She wasn't the only one who wondered about your gender. It was the first question people wondered or asked about you! Which would you be: a rascally little boy or a precious little girl? In fact, at the news of a baby's birth, people will typically ask, "What is it?" before they ask, "Is the baby healthy?"

What's more, everyone who meets you every day of your life following your birth will note immediately whether you are male or female. Every one of us immediately begins to form opinions, questions, and thoughts based upon gender. You do the same with everyone you meet, most likely without even being aware of it. No one has ever said, "You know, I didn't even notice if that person was a man or a woman." When you tell about hearing the most captivating speaker the other day or meeting the nicest person on a trip, you genderize the details without even noticing. It's no small part of the story you are telling.

What I want us to consider is *why*.

We do this because knowing a person's sex is our first effort to *understand* and *identify*, to *connect*. As humans, we are made to ask, *What is it?* We intuitively organize everything into appropriate categories. With children, we can't initially know whether he will be more analytical or creative, what sort of humor she will have, what his personality will be, or what career she might pursue. But we can know what gender a child is, and most parents would agree it's a pretty important fact to know at the start. Knowing if we are having a little boy or a little girl means so much more than what color we will paint the nursery. Regardless of our views on gender, our children's sex determines how we'll interact with them, what we'll do or not do with them, and how they will understand and identify us.

Recently, our oldest daughter, Olivia, had her first crush over to our house. The two of them made pizza for the family, and it was a milestone event for all of us. Our youngest daughter, Isabel, is a second grader. She excitedly asked if Michael was staying for a sleepover. For Isabel, that's what good friends do on special evenings—they stay up late watching movies and then they sleep over. Why would this be any different?

Well, because of gender. Gender matters, and in countless different ways.

Think about how this works itself out in adulthood. At a final job interview, this time with the CEO, an interviewee has made a good impression. After offering the position to the candidate, the CEO extends this invitation: "Listen, I've a got a beautiful new Catalina 470 and my family doesn't like sailing. How'd you like to join me next weekend out at the Cape?"

A nice invitation and great opportunity. But what if the CEO is a woman and the new employee a married man, or vice versa? Sex differences would completely change the nature of the invitation from friendly to awkward or even a bit creepy. Imagine a woman coming home to tell her husband about the new job and the sailing invitation. No doubt, he will care quite deeply about the male-female question, and he'd be legitimately concerned if his wife wasn't. This is universally true.

In my day job at Focus on the Family, I handle a good share of calls from media on various issues relating to gender identity and the family. More than one reporter has asked if gender is really that important in parenting. Many believe the popular but false line that children just need loving and caring parents.

"I hear your busy newsroom in the background," I respond. "Say it was staffed exclusively by men. How different do you think the environment and your publication would be if that were the case? Doesn't a great publication like yours simply need smart and talented journalists, regardless of sex difference?"

Usually I hear a nervous chuckle, followed by a sheepish, "I get your point." If a newspaper, magazine, or television news program needs distinctive gender-specific input and influence, how much more does the family that is generated by these differences? In most given human situations, it's silly to believe gender makes no meaningful difference.

Male and female matter! The argument that says otherwise is merely a cultural construction of the past few decades.

DIFFERENCE MAKES ALL THE DIFFERENCE

Let's now consider the importance of differences. Difference is what makes the world work. Consider the book you're holding. The contrast of the black ink on the white page makes it work. It's simple, but profound. The cooperative contrast of these two different elements creates something useful. No one asks, "Why can't we work for more similarity between the print and the page?" The power and effectiveness of the print and page is in their complete contrast and difference and in the way they work together—the same kind of dissimilarity that makes electricity work, cars run, airplanes fly, bicycles go, doors lock, knives cut, atoms spin, and electrons fire. This sophisticated computer I'm writing on—and those that now run the world—works by the simple distinction of ones and zeros.

Difference makes the world work.

Think of how God explains His account of creation. He does so by distinction—light and darkness, water and sky, and so on. The first thing we learn in the Bible is that God is distinct from creation; in the beginning God *was* and creation *was not*. Then God created, and it was. *Distinct!*

God's first creative act is really separation and distinction: light from darkness (see Genesis 1:3–5). Next, water from sky, then sea from land. God continues this dividing and contrasting in the creatures of the sea and the air, the animals of the land, and finally, man, different and distinct from the animals (see verses 24–30). This is how God explains the world to us, with whom He shares it.

Then humanity is given a profound distinction. The first chapter of Scripture tells us that after five days of creating, God declares He would make something with a grand uniqueness: it will bear His image, giving the created world a tangible and experiential picture of the invisible and immeasurable God. He says, "Let Us make man in Our image, according to Our likeness" (verse 26).

As splendid as all of creation was—the clown fish, the gazelle, the panda, the millipede, the peregrine falcon, the sunflower, the coral reefs—how could God best represent His own splendor in a created being?

God tells us plainly: "So God created man in His own image; in the image of God He created him; male and female He created them" (verse 27).

Male and female! Are you one of these? If so, you just learned the most profound truth about yourself—and your gender—that you could know. It describes you and all those around you, forever shaping how you receive and treat them.

Both man and woman *are* uniquely the earthly image of the invisible God. The distinguished scholar Leon Kass, from the University of Chicago, illuminates the importance of this word *image* in his careful study of Genesis, where he notes the Hebrew word translated "image" is *tselem*, from a root meaning "to cut off," "to chisel"; literally, something cut or chiseled out. This word brings to mind a sculpture representing something greater. The artist of the sculpture is saying to us, "Look at this that I am creating and be reminded of something larger, the bigger *something* it stands for. Something worth knowing about." Kass says,

> Any image, insofar as it is an image, has a most peculiar manner of being: it both *is* and *is not* what it resembles. The image of my granddaughter that smiles at me out of the picture frame on my desk *is* my granddaughter—not yours. But it is *not* really she— just a *mere* image. Although being merely a likeness, an image not only resembles but also points to, and is dependent for its very being on, that of which it is an image. Man, like any other creature, is simply what he is. But according to the text [of Genesis], he is—in addition—also something more insofar as he resembles the divine.[2] (emphasis in the original)

We are all image bearers of the Divine. And don't miss this point: It is our *gendered* humanity that images God. God was certain to make that clear on the first page of His Word to us, and it can't be missed: "In the image of God He created him; male and female He created them."

Any observer can tell that man and woman are different without even trying because of this deeply divine distinction—a distinction that shows us something important about the nature of God. We can't fully understand *how* this is, but we know *that* it is.

Understanding how we grow children into healthy men and women is certainly about healthy human development, but it's about *so* much more. Because God is imaged in male and female, raising boys and girls is a deeply divine task. This first human truth that we are either male or female is a central part of the divine story.

The beautiful, passionate, and intimate contrast and cooperation of male and female is the door we all pass through to get to where we are today. Humanity is like an elite country club: you have to know someone on the inside to get in. We call these special connections *parents*. Both must be involved in your entrance, because the hard-and-fast, nonnegotiable rule of the club is clear: no mom, no dad, no entrance. Every one of us is a living testimony to the importance and beauty of the essential cooperation between male and female.

The End Game of Parenting

My desire is to help you teach your child to navigate between the two extreme views of gender identity that are present in our culture today. One group firmly believes that the way you nurture or socialize a child trumps the work of nature; the other demands that no amount of nurture should change the inborn wild-at-heart or captivating nature of boys and girls.

Our definition of gender has to involve both nature and nurture to truly explain the essential difference and how we authentically live in our humanity throughout distinct cultures of the world. Our natures are real, but so are our nurturing environments. If not, parenting would simply be about providing food, clothing, and shelter.

I love what Dorothy Boyd (played by Renée Zellweger) in the movie *Jerry Maguire* says about raising her little boy without a father. She says all her girlfriends are out "trying to get a man. Trying to keep a man. Not me, I'm trying to raise a man!"

Here's a mom who knows what her end game is. Just how do we take these new members of this prestigious humanity club who come to us as boys or girls and turn them into happy, well-adjusted men and women?

Proverbs 22:6 exhorts parents to "train a child in the way he should go, and when he is old he will not turn from it" (NIV). Solomon tells us two things here:

1. How we train a child will affect the kind of adult he
   or she grows into.
2. There is a way *each* child should go.

It's not just that there is one path that's right for all children. This is certainly true when we think of qualities like truthfulness, compassion, and diligence—these apply to everyone. But it also means there's a way that *each* child should go! God makes every one of us distinct individuals. He doesn't use a mold. And He delights in this individuality. Our job as parents is to honor that uniqueness and nurture it. Parent, raise your child in the way *he* or *she* should go, not the way they do it next door or like some group at church or those impressive camps or schools. They are not raising *your* child. Your job is to pay attention to the way this unique little person should be going. For God has a unique and important life for your child to live.

How can you possibly raise a gender-secure son or daughter if you don't know what the end game looks like? Who starts out on a journey simply hoping and trusting they'll arrive without considering the destination and how to get there? I'm convinced parents today are worse off than at any other time in human history because of the doubts the world has placed in our minds about the importance and even the existence of sex distinction.

I write this book as a much-needed and realistic guide, out of my fifteen years of experience as a full-time researcher in family-strengthening work, where I have carefully examined the social and psychological sciences on how mothers and fathers contribute to healthy child development. But I also write it out of my practical experience of more than twenty-seven years of marriage and raising five children with my wife. I have a deep and personal interest in this topic for myself, for our children, and for my friends and family members who are parents as well.

Our gender distinction carries profound meaning in God's story. So

I share from both a personal and professional perspective, informed by both science and theology, which really do affirm each other.

Unfortunately, the issue of gender distinction has become a politically loaded topic. Too many people have bought into the notion that *different* means *unequal* and that the only way to increase the standing of women in society is to downplay the differences between male and female. However, I don't understand how it elevates women to make them more like men and to make men more like women. The fact is, women have great power, influence, and intuition that men don't have, while men have powers, influences, and ways of looking at life that women don't have. This truth is beneficial to both and empowers both.

Which is better? Are fruits more important than vegetables? Is sunshine more important than rain? Both are most important, just like male and female. We can't sustain a civil and productive culture without both.

My intention is not to upset people. If the rhetoric of political correctness keeps us from exploring the issue of gender differences, we lose something valuable to our humanity. Amazing scientific evidences of essential sex difference in the fields of anthropology, psychology, endocrinology, and neurology in the last few decades strongly disprove nearly all the thinking that drove the misunderstandings about gender in the first place. In fact, the more sophisticated this scientific research gets, the more it deepens our insight into the importance of male and female differences and how profoundly they exist within us.

Aren't Boys and Girls More Similar than Different?

I often hear that while all this "difference stuff" might be true, men and women are more similar than different. I readily agree. They are both human, no small fact. Each is a thinking and feeling being with two arms and two legs who walks upright. They both show emotion and speak to communicate ideas and desires. Both will laugh, cry, and experience sadness. They both find enjoyment in working and relaxing. There are hundreds of ways men and women are similar.

But many things are more similar than different, yet their variations and distinctions carry significance. Consider salt and sugar, a horse and a zebra. Imagine giving Johnny Cash a ukulele just before he goes on stage at Folsom Prison and telling him everything's cool because it's more similar to a guitar than it is different.

Small differences can indeed make all the difference! Dr. Louann Brizendine, a neuropsychiatrist at the University of California in San Francisco, explains this similarity-difference issue nicely in her excellent book *The Female Brain*:

> More than 99 percent of male and female genetic coding is exactly the same. Out of the thirty thousand genes in the human genome, the less than one percent variation between the sexes is small. But that percentage difference influences *every single cell in our bodies*—from the nerves that register pleasure and pain to the neurons that transmit perception, thoughts, feelings, and emotions.[3] (emphasis added)

What Is Essentially Male or Female?

So what are the distinctive qualities of the human male and female? This monumental question is one well worth considering, and I hope to help us understand the answers. However, to keep us from being disappointed in any collection of qualities, we need to recognize that answering this question demands a very big view. No list or description could pretend to capture *every* aspect of masculinity or femininity. Others could come up with genuine qualities that I leave out. But a substantive, respectable, and descriptive collection of genuine and largely universal man and woman qualities can be assembled, and I try to do that in this book.

So I invite you to read on with an open mind. Briefly, here's what lies ahead:

- Chapters 1 and 2 describe the distinctly and largely cross-cultural male and female qualities boys and girls possess.

- Chapters 3 and 4 explore how parents reinforce masculine and feminine qualities in their sons and daughters.

- Chapters 5 and 6 look at these gender-distinct qualities, exploring how we want our sons and daughters to turn out as men and women and what we can do to help them get there.

- Chapters 7–13 examine how the same male-female qualities in us as moms and dads contribute a broad array of necessary things in the healthy development of our children's well-being, security, compassion, confidence, intellect, and maturity.

- Chapter 14 explores how gender differences affect your marriage and how you can use that wonderful difference to raise amazing children.

- Finally, for those who want to dig a little deeper, the appendix provides additional and fascinating scientific data that point to the important gender differences in men and women across diverse human cultures.

As you take in and weigh all of this information, my prayer for you is twofold: first, that you will gain a deeper understanding of the God-given differences between male and female that exist in wonderful and mysterious ways in your children; and second, that you will gain an appreciation for how gender distinctions between you and your spouse provide essential contributions to the growth and maturity of your developing boys and girls.

Raising secure daughters and confident sons is, by definition, gender-distinct work. It's the most important work going on in the world, and the next generation and those following are counting on us to get it right.

PART I

A *Clear Vision* for Authentic Manhood *and* Womanhood— and *How to Help* Your Kids Get There

ONE

What Makes a Good Man?

Your little boy grows, survives puberty, and is now closing in on age eighteen. After school and weekends, he works at the Apple Store at the upscale mall on the edge of town. It's his first job, and he loves that it allows him to demonstrate his dual gifts of instantly comprehending the latest computer applications and putting people at ease while helping them understand new technology. He's thriving in his first significant grown-up role beyond your home, and you couldn't be more proud.

You're eager to visit him at work, meet his supervisors, and see him in action in his new world, so you anxiously wait until he gives the cue. The evening comes when your son says his favorite manager will be working and this would be the best time to come. You casually stroll into the store, browse around, and wait for your son to finish with a customer. In the meantime, your son's manager approaches you, asking if he can help you with anything. You and your spouse introduce yourselves and explain you're only in the market to see your son's new workplace. The manager tells you how happy he is to have your son on his team. He praises your son for being a fast learner, a good listener, and always ready to help out with the most mundane tasks. He comments on how he wishes all his younger employees were as mature, conscientious, and willing to learn as your son. He ends by telling you you've raised a fine young man.

You and your spouse trade a covert fist bump with your eyes. You thank the manager for his kind words.

If you've experienced something like this from a friend, a coach, or a teacher, you've tasted one of the sweetest rewards of good parenting: having another adult comment on how your son is growing, maturing, and headed in the direction toward becoming a good man.

"What a fine young man" or "He's a good boy" are some of the best words a parent can hear. Yet when you think about those statements, you know what "fine" and "good" mean, but what about "man" or "boy"? What does it really mean to be a good *man*? What is a healthy *boy*? Are there specific qualities that describe healthy masculinity and don't apply as much or at all to women?

Boys and men are fascinating creatures. Don't you think the world becomes a better, happier, and healthier place when men are encouraged to become the best version of who they already are? That's part of our job as parents raising boys. Still, we are wise to remember that Clint Eastwood is not Albert Einstein is not Harrison Ford is not George Washington Carver is not Abraham Lincoln is not Bill Gates is not LeBron James is not Mark Twain is not Bob Dylan is not Conan O'Brien is not Teddy Roosevelt is not your husband or your son.

Yet each of these and a million other men will exhibit many distinctly male qualities. Of course, we need to remember that not all boys or men will tend toward *all* of these male qualities, nor will they exhibit the qualities in the *same* ways. But this doesn't make them any less male, nor does it mean we can't speak meaningfully about what *male* is. Each male is an individual male, because that's the way it works.

With all this in mind, let's make some observations about the qualities of boys and men—the essentials that make them males.

Men Are Explorative

The statement wasn't, "Go west, young lady!"

"Almost every man you know is on a quest," explains Michael Gurian, one of the world's leading thinkers on what boys and men are really about.[1] He explains that a girl's self-worth and life connection is inherently found within herself. But for men, it is a different story. Gurian explains that the man must "earn his meaning. Boys know this from very early on, turning their eyes outward into the world, seeking new experiences and challenges through which they experience their hidden potencies, earn a sense of self-worth, and gain importance."[2]

Consider the male's unique physical orientation: it's more outward, penetrative, seeking. A man's destiny lies "out there" somewhere. He won't find it within himself. His male essence points him beyond! He must get up, prepare himself, rouse his confidence, and go to it. This is true in finding a girl, his destiny, and everything else your boy seeks in life. If you remember anything about parenting a son, this reality of his exploratory nature contains it.

A man is a being on a quest. He must seek his fortune that lies beyond, and he won't stop until he finds it. Think of any classic story where a young man leaves the homestead to find his life somewhere else—the prince in search of true love, the son in search of fortune.

Your boy must be both *taught* and *allowed* to explore. I understand this with my own son, and I try to help Jackie appreciate it. Schaeffer must be able to go just a bit beyond the boundaries of our neighborhood when he reaches the proper age. This is an important part of his development as a confident male—both to actually do it but also to know his parents have confidence in his ability to do it.

Out there is where a man finds what he needs, where his destiny lies. And he must go, pressing through to find it. This is his undeniable nature.

MEN ARE DETERMINED TO DELIVER THE GOODS

Once a man finds his destiny—whether his bride or his life's calling—he needs to be confident knowing he can accomplish the task at hand. Humanity depends on it. A vast advertising and pharmaceutical industry centers on helping men ensure they'll be able to deliver the goods when the opportunity calls. Wanting to accomplish the task at hand holds true for the sexual act as well as everything else in life for men.

This quality also explains why boys and men are so fascinated with tools and gadgets and why they'll buy the most seemingly senseless devices. They might just need to fix a pipe or a gasket, and they can't be found without the right tool when that time arises.

You probably remember the amazing and lifesaving emergency landing of US Airways Flight 1549 in the icy waters of the Hudson River. The world rightfully praised the pilot, Captain C.B. "Sully" Sullenberger, for bringing what was needed to the task. Captain Sullenberger certainly doesn't fit the stereotypical masculine image physically. But in a much deeper and authentic place, he's "got the goods." Of course, the rest of the flight crew performed their tasks heroically, both men and women. But Sully was indisputably "the man," because his confidence and calm made everyone else's service possible.

The same quality is found in the little boy working with his Lincoln

Logs, building a fort until way after dark, or creating an art project. Don't tell him that finishing isn't important, that he's done enough, or that he can start again tomorrow. He's got to finish it now! A boy, just like a man, has to see it through.

At the same time, boys can also be easily distracted, quickly moving on to the next thing. (We address this next.) A healthy balance between obsession and distraction is essential. Living between the two is what boys need as they learn and grow into healthy, well-balanced men.

Men Need to Know What's Next

The man seldom lingers. Left to himself, he is more likely to do whatever he needs to do and move on to the next thing. A sandwich and television are most likely the next thing. Cuddling is not.

I recall coming home from work one day to find that Jackie had re-arranged the living room. When I walked in, I noticed the changes and immediately told her I liked what she'd done. I *really* did like it. It was a smart redesign and I told her so. She did an amazing job and I came to that conclusion instantly.

After my comments, she asked if I liked the lamp better on the foyer table or on the desk. I told her the table was perfect and then went right upstairs to change my clothes. Later, she came up and I could tell something was bothering her, but I had no idea what. When I asked what was wrong, she said that I didn't seem interested in what she had done in the living room. Honestly shocked, I told her I really did like it much better than before. Since I had already said as much when I was downstairs, I couldn't help but think, *What in the world about that was the wrong thing to do?*

It turned out that she didn't really want to know where the lamp looked best. Instead, she was excited to talk about the possibilities *with* me and bring me into the process. She wanted me to join her in her world. She wanted to cuddle, so to speak—to linger in the satisfaction of her work. Job done, I had quickly moved on to the next thing, which was changing out of my work clothes. She felt ignored even though from my male perspective I clearly had not ignored her. A woman's emotional currency is different and a good man might not *feel* it, but he should try to be aware of it.

For the man, an event is something that gets him to the next thing. For the woman, the event is the thing. Boys need to be taught to be content in the now, but we also need to understand their wiring is deeply directed at what comes next and that they are driven to go after it. It might seem impatient and erratic to mom, but there is something really "guy" there and it needs to be nurtured and properly directed.

At the same time, boys need to find their "chill" setting. If on one day out of the week God rested, reflected, and didn't move on to the next thing, then men can too.

MEN ARE OPPORTUNISTS

The man doesn't usually need feelings, setting, or reasons. He just needs the urge and the opportunity. The opportunist is always looking for what's next, and men will tend to be more impulsive in some ways than women. Why is car insurance for young men most expensive? A wandering man will fall into an affair much faster than a woman, perhaps in an evening. Cross-cultural research reveals that this is true for men across the world in very different cultures and settings. Men as a rule are much more interested in having sex with a strange woman they just met than a woman is with a strange man.[3] Fortunately, the research also indicates that 60 to 75 percent of men around the world are faithful to their spouses.

Opportunism can have good and bad sides. Tiger Woods sought both good and bad opportunities—some on the course and others elsewhere. A good man seeks opportunities by thinking with his head and sometimes his heart. A stupid man doesn't think. Healthy masculinity knows to say, "Git 'er done," to the right opportunities and flee the wrong ones without giving them any thought.

MEN MUST TAKE CHANCES

As a man goes out to find his opportunity and deliver the goods, he faces the possibility that he might fail. He might be shot down or fail to live up to performance requirements. This is what the main story in the movie *Hitch* was about. The nerdy low guy on the totem pole wants desperately to approach one of the wealthiest and most beautiful women in New York. When Hitch (Will Smith), the dating coach, hears this, he tells his new client, Albert Brennamen (Kevin James), "Man, you *really* swing for the fence, don't you?"

A healthy, confident man has to aim for the fence, knowing he could go down swinging. He has to take the chance, even at the risk of embarrassing himself. All boys and men must learn to become comfortable taking chances. If not, they won't ever get anything meaningful done. Both failure and rejection lurk around every corner. But so do opportunities.

Some people made fun of Fred Rogers—of *Mister Rogers' Neighborhood*—during the height of his career as not being a good role model of masculinity because of his gentle manner. But in my opinion he was quite masculine—not in the stereotypical way, but in the genuine way he charted his own course as a man in daytime children's television and didn't look back. He took a chance and, like Sinatra, did it his way. That's pretty macho!

Boys must be taught to take calculated and smart chances: to climb a little higher in the tree, to jump off things of reasonable height, and to ride their bikes a little bit faster. Safety comes not in keeping them from these things but in teaching them how to take the right chances reasonably.

MEN ARE INITIATORS

Being the initiator is closely linked to being the chance taker and the explorer. In nearly all cultures, the male is the initiator.

The most obvious example of this is seen in sexual terms. Women will certainly make their interests and desires known, and men benefit from knowing how to read the subtle invitations correctly. But the man initiates. Sometimes his initiation is exactly the right thing at the right time. Other times, not so much. But it's the male's nature to keep trying. He can't *not* do so.

This quality applies to much more than making sex happen. Young boys need to learn how to gain the confidence, judgment, and insight to make the right thing happen at the right time that serves others or gets something good and meaningful accomplished. Boys need to be encouraged to initiate good things like, "Hey, let's start a neighborhood kickball league! We can have regular games at four o'clock every day and divide up the teams fairly. We can make team shirts and use that field over there!" This is what boys will and should do: offer the initiative and leadership to get good things started and see them through.

This is where business leaders and founders of institutions learn what they need to launch important enterprises. Of course, girls and women also can show great leadership, but this quality should be carefully and more intentionally developed in boys because it's a deeper part of their nature.

Men Are Active and Aggressive

Again, this quality is most clear in terms of sexuality. The male is by far the more active player. While the female is anything but passive, the male is more likely to work up the greater sweat.

Michael Gurian explains that the brain chemical vasopressin is why "sexual activity in men is, at its baseline, an aggression activity."[4] During foreplay, this chemical is secreted in the male. It's what drives the man to *want* the woman: to take her, to have her, to make his existence and power known to her sexually. Gurian explains that at an animal level, vasopressin is the driver in territorial marking and sexual dominance. And it is male.

What does this have to do with boys? Plenty. Neuropsychiatrist Louann Brizendine explains that the male brain is two and a half times larger and more vital in the center devoted to aggression and action.[5] After puberty, your son's brain will have two times more space dedicated to sexual drive than your daughter's brain.

Boys are inclined to be active. The part of the brain that registers threat and aggression response, the amygdala, is also much larger in the male brain, which explains why many boys can go from zero to fight in less than sixty seconds. A friend told me recently that when his son was about fifteen, he had to have his wrist pinned in surgery. When he was coming out of the anesthesia, he started punching at an invisible nemesis, which the ER nurse said is very common for teen boys.

It's the male's nature to be physically active. On an episode of the NBC comedy *The Office,* the police have set up a mobile speed detector in front of the office to signal drivers when they're going too fast. The men see it from the office window and immediately head down to the street in the middle of their workday to take turns running as fast as they can past the detector's beam to see who can register the highest speed. While this is also about competition, the physicality of the game is what is enticing for men. Physical activity is a difficult thing for males to resist because it's part of their nature.

Boys need to learn the proper balance between displaying their active nature and demonstrating self-control. Cutting work to run past the speed detector is fine sometimes. But do it too often and you might find yourself with all kinds of free time for such activities. Boys need to have this part of their nature both encouraged and governed to be exhibited in the right ways at the right times. Boys whose aggressive nature is not both affirmed and directed in healthy ways, particularly by their fathers, are the kind of boys who grow up to make sure others recognize their "strength" through violence and guns.

MEN ARE COMPETITIVE AND DOMINANT

Men want the best and will expend incredible energy toward getting it. They secure their self-esteem by successfully competing for the best girl in the room and other victories.

Boys need to learn to be comfortable with competition, because it's where they get a great deal of their esteem and where they learn to lose and win with graciousness. They don't always have to win to gain confidence, but they need to believe they're at least making progress. I never could beat my dad wrestling until I was much older. Of course, by then I didn't need to. But when I was young, I would get closer to pinning him each year, and that was good for me. I just needed to keep trying. There's a big lesson here: boys should learn to be dominant, but in the proper way with both confidence and gentleness.

Think of Christ as a wonderful example. He was certainly in control, very commanding, yet He was a matchless model of servanthood. From childhood, Jesus grew in strength and insight; even the very old teachers in the temple courts were deeply impressed with His knowledge and understanding far beyond His years (see Luke 2:40, 47). In His adult ministry, Jesus never manipulated or intimidated His followers with His strength and power. He served, but with confidence and authority.

One of the most important aspects of parenting boys is teaching them this important balance between confident, healthy dominance and selfless, tender service. Think of men in your own family, at church, on sports teams, or in your circle of friends who represent this well. A real-life example is powerful and instructive. Make sure your boy knows what kind of models represent the balance he should look for in his life and which ones to avoid.

YOUR AMAZING BOY

As parents, we need to realize that our boys need help, encouragement, and guidance on the inevitable road to male adulthood so they become authentic, healthy, vibrant, virtuous, and wise males in their

- exploration
- deliver the goods
- moving to the next thing
- opportunism
- chance taking
- initiative
- activity
- competition and dominance

Your job as a parent is to raise your boy to be the man he was created to be. In addition to being aware of the masculine traits we've explored, you need to pay attention to three key co-instructors—and not necessarily in this order:

1. The examples of men around you, both good and bad. Become an attentive student of them with your boy. Study what is virtuously male and what is not.

2. The nature, temperament, and passions of the boy God has entrusted to you. God didn't make him in a mold but designed him to grow to be a special, unique man. And the clues to who that man is can be found in the boy he is today. Pay attention to what those might be.

3. The Creator's intentions for His creation. Both parents must be mindful of God's prompting and direction in raising this unique boy whom He created for a special purpose. And God gave different and complementary insights to both mom and dad as sex-distinct parents. Allow both to have a say in his development and formation.

HEALTHY BALANCE

The key to many things in life is balance. We need to recognize and remember that there are healthy manifestations of the masculine qualities we've discussed as well as unhealthy ones.

A competitive spirit can send your son to the top and drive him to accomplish important things. But being too competitive will ensure he's lonely at the top as a despised winner. Who wants that? Similarly, there's a distinction between healthy humility and passivity, between confident boldness and arrogance. Your boy should learn the desirable qualities from you and be able to discern the ugly ones. The task of both mothers and fathers is to help their children learn the healthy emphasis and balance of these universal male qualities.

As we close, I want to insert an important note. There *is* an authentic masculinity that most men will exhibit in similar and different ways. As you raise your son, you want to think about what kind of man, husband, and father your remarkable little boy should grow into. In order to set those important objectives, you need to know some of the most important universal masculine qualities that are true of men around the world in different cultures throughout time. Also, be mindful of the strong body of research indicating that when a relationship between a boy and his father is loving and warm, as opposed to critical and stoic, those boys are indeed more likely to develop healthily in more masculine ways.[6]

Good men seldom develop naturally. Anthropologists who have studied very diverse cultures—modern and ancient, remote and central—explain that each culture must intentionally teach boys to become good men, more so than in teaching girls to become women.[7] Men have to be made, and our culture needs all the good men it can get. In particular, your son's future wife and children need one good man.

As parents of a boy, you are very much in the man-building business. It is critically important and deeply rewarding work that the world needs.

We have two boys, three years apart. The older one could be described as all boy through and through. But our younger son, age four, is much more gentle, quiet, and sensitive. Should we expect him to be more like his older brother?

You should only expect him to be like his older brother in that both should be kind, obey, and keep their elbows off the table! Any two boys will be different because God made them that way. Yours are clearly different little boys and should be allowed to be different.

However, in light of what you have described, both boys need some things. Your rough-and-tumble son needs to learn to channel his energy in safe and proper ways. It's fine for him to jump from the top tier of the jungle gym, but he can't do so if it means landing on top of the kids playing below. We all need to control our God-given energy so that we or others don't get hurt.

You can affirm your younger son in his quietness and sensitivity, but he can learn to display those qualities in masculine ways. What might that look like? No one thinks of Yo-Yo Ma as a mama's boy because he's a creative artist, labels Mikhail Baryshnikov a nancy boy for being a dancer, or views Emeril Lagasse as less manly because he likes to spend most of his time in the kitchen creating beautiful cuisine. There are masculine ways to do seemingly feminine things.

One mom told me she was concerned that her eight-year-old boy was excited about some pretty flowers they came upon. She didn't want to meet his request that she take his picture standing in the front of the flowers. His excitement about their beauty was a just a little too unmasculine for her.

I asked her if she thought another approach might work. She could talk with him about why the flowers fascinated him and get him to explore that reaction. She might tell him about botanists who study flowers, and she could look for a good male role model in this field, such as John Bartram. This gentle guidance can help him learn to develop his interests in a healthy masculine way.

My three-year-old likes to play dress up with his sisters. But I'm concerned because he likes to dress up in the same dresses his sisters wear. And he loves wearing their sparkly shoes. How can I stop this?

First of all, understand that this behavior at age three isn't *necessarily* concerning. Your son is at the age where he's starting to recognize and appreciate the differences between boys and girls and what they do and wear. So dressing up this way in play can be simply how he relates to and plays with his sisters.

Instead of panicking, you can steer him gently toward more boy-type dress-up clothes. Ask him what he would like, giving him some ideas to draw from, such as firemen, cowboys, karate fighters, and so on. The key at his age is not to react, but merely to guide and direct gently.

The dad can and should play a key role here. For boys, mom should be the "corrector," the one who says, "No, boys don't act like that." Dad should be the "inviter," the one who says, "Hey, buddy, when I was a boy, I loved to dress up like a safari hunter," and then lead him in that direction. Let the boy have the opportunity to be welcomed and invited into his father's world of manhood by his father.

This is critical, because no boy has ever been successfully scolded into the world of manhood by his father. It's always by invitation and encouragement.

———

I'm a single mom, and I appreciate what you're saying about what a healthy male looks like. I know this is important for my two boys, ages six and ten. How can I encourage this kind of development without a man around?

You've already overcome your biggest hurdle: realizing that while a mom can certainly help her boys become healthy men, she does have limitations. She is not a man. So here are a couple of ideas:

Option 1: You and your sons have access to good men at church and in your neighborhood as well as with uncles and grandfathers in your extended family. Explore how your sons can spend time with some of these men, doing various tasks, from simply running errands to building a doghouse. Often, the best and most healthy times boys can spend with men come in doing the most unglamorous things, like changing a flat tire.

Also, for teaching purposes you can draw on men you don't even know. With your boys, actively observe men you encounter in books, movies, shows, and everyday life. Talk about the kinds of men they are and if their behavior is worth emulating. Explore why. When men you observe display those manly flaws of arrogance, anger, and selfishness, ask your boys how they would improve themselves if they acted that way. You'll be amazed at what your sons can learn from these conversations. Your opinions about these men can be very influential as well, because you're communicating not only what is masculine but also what is attractive or desirable to women—particularly to you, the most important woman in their young lives.

Option 2: You might be a single parent, but there is a man in your sons' lives, even if only in their imagination. This man—their father—might be long gone due to desertion or death. Or he might be in and out of their lives from month to month. Or perhaps he has regular healthy contact with them.

In any of these situations, your boys have an image of their dad in their minds. You can use this image as a teaching device to help them understand what healthy masculinity is. If he's chosen not to be on the scene, you don't have to dog the man. But you can talk honestly about the pain his actions have caused in your family's life and whether such behavior is a mark of a good man. Ask your sons how they might do better than their dad. If your sons' father is deceased, they have the gift of his memory and reputation to guide them. Talk often about what their father liked to do and how he handled certain situations well and the admirable qualities he lived out.

TWO

What Makes a Good Woman?

One of the greatest wonders in my life is having the privilege and responsibility of raising four amazing daughters. I love being a dad to our girls. They are such sweeties, and I value the special impact a father can have in the lives of his daughters.

When our first child, Olivia, was born, I fell head over heels in love with this amazing, miraculous little creature God had entrusted to us. I'd play with her for hours, and I was happy to change her diapers, feed her, or do anything else that allowed me to interact with her. I would push her in the stroller on long walks around the neighborhood nearly every day, talking about everything we saw. I talked, she listened. As she grew, we spent hours and hours at the park near our house. That's where I taught her to walk. Those years passed far too quickly. Now she's an amazing, beautiful, wise, hilarious, godly sixteen-year-old young woman. I'm both humbled and amazed at how well she is turning out. She is getting wise enough to give me keen insight when I ask her for advice. I do this for two reasons: I have come to trust her judgment, and she needs to know that she possesses that quality. This builds great things into her.

My second daughter is Sophia, the twin sister of our only son, Schaeffer. Sophie emerged from the womb smiling, just happy to be a part of the scene, and she has remained that way. I'm amazed at how kind she is to everyone as she grows in her early teen years. She gets that from her mom. Sophie was also our doll girl. She *loved* baby dolls and was on the verge of becoming like the crazy cat lady. She couldn't get enough. She had names, stories, routines, and likes and dislikes for all her babies, and she never got their stories mixed up. I once told her I noticed that she was always caring for the babies alone, without the help of her husband. "Where is he?" I asked. With a roll of her eyes, she told me he works all the time. Having so many babies required that he work two jobs. I told her I was glad to have such a conscientious son-in-law. I asked what he did at these two jobs. Sophie explained he was a professional baseball player and pizza delivery man. When I asked which job kept him traveling around the country so much, she answered, "Oh, it's his pizza delivery job."

Tess was our little surprise baby, as well as quite a little prize. We can count on one hand the number of times she had a good crying fit during her first four or five years. She was always a contented baby, usually with an infectious smile on her face. She was also a solid little rock—built Ford tough. Her heart is tender, and she'll tell you she's all "girly girl." Jackie and I have to be careful because she is very compliant and eager to serve, so we are more likely to reactively ask her to help with little favors around the house. She also isn't one to look out for herself, so she can easily and unwittingly get rolled over by the others too.

Our baby is Isabel. I've told her that when she is an adult and has babies of her own, she will *still* be my baby. She loves to play outside with the neighborhood girls, and as the senior among the little girls on our street, she's keen to make sure she is a good role model for them. She's the family champion at Mario Kart Wii, without playing it all that much. She just gets it. She's an amazing reader, and when we snuggle in her bed at night for her to read to me, she always wants to read "just one more page, please?" *Caps for Sale* is our current favorite.

I find joy in raising our girls because I have the opportunity to help build four amazing women who we'll send into society to make a difference. As their dad, I won't allow anyone to make them feel small about themselves. Each knows the Eleanor Roosevelt quote, "No one can make you feel inferior without your consent." I think smart, confident, and capable women who love both God and others provide a great gift to the world. I'm humbled that God has entrusted me with these four incredible young women.

Of course, to raise good, strong, and caring women, we must know what the qualities of a woman are. Without that, we have no clear objective or destination. If we talk about the qualities of a good woman without employing authentically feminine descriptors, we're simply describing a good human being. That's not a bad thing, because being human is no small thing. But to be human *is* to be gendered. And to deny our gender is to deny our humanity.

We want to be sure we examine qualities that are universally feminine and not merely cultural, because this helps us get to the core of what true femininity means. Remember, your daughter might not exhibit all of these and she might not exhibit them in the ways other girls do. But these qualities do help us understand what it is to be a woman. Of course, your daughter is a unique being—no one else is like her. As parents, we are wise to remember that Emily Dickinson is not Aretha Franklin is not Clara Barton is not Flannery O'Connor is not Harriet Tubman is not Julia Roberts is not Rachel Ray is not Condoleezza Rice is not Amelia

Earhart is not Jane Goodall is not Katharine Hepburn is not Margaret Thatcher is not Beatrix Potter is not Carole King is not Tina Fey is not Sarah Palin is not Jane Austen is not your wife or your daughter. Your daughter is uniquely designed, and she is depending on you to help shape, mold, and guide her into womanhood.

So what are the authentic qualities of a woman? What is her essence? What is your sweet daughter moving toward, and how can you help guide her toward that goal in healthy ways?

WOMEN ARE CONFIDENTLY ENTICING

"A girl is born with an inherent, directly natural path to self-worth," Michael Gurian explains. "Nature has provided her with a natural calling and intimately biological legacy."[1] Unlike the male who must go out into the world to find his destiny and opportunity, the woman possesses her future within herself. She has a hidden but deep confidence in this.

A woman isn't as inclined to look outward for her life. She is naturally and fundamentally introspective. This explains why phrases like, "Let's talk about our relationship," or, "You don't seem to connect with my feelings," can strike fear into the heart of men but come more naturally to women. He's not centered that way; she is.

Her fundamental physical orientation is to take in and nurture. As such, she entices. While this word *entice* has gotten a negative reputation, in its true womanly form, to entice confidently means to know where the center of your life is and to know what you want. The woman knows what she wants, and she draws it to herself. Too few women today understand what incredible power they hold in this.

Ask any man who is married to a confident woman if he pursued her because she indicated through some subtle but unmistakable sign that she was interested in and open to him. My former boss, Dr. James Dobson, has told how he and his wife, Shirley, met. He was headed across their college campus to play tennis one afternoon when she called to him from across the lawn, "Hey, legs!" She was sending a clear message, and in time he got it. He made the next move, and there you go!

Women also do this with their children. From the first moment of their lives, the mother draws them to herself. Rare is the adult who complains that he or she didn't have a close relationship with mom. Few suffer from what we call a "mother wound" as they do from a "father wound." Motherlessness is not a social problem like fatherlessness. Mom doesn't have to decide to become relational. That's who she *is*.

WOMEN SEEK INTIMACY OVER ACTION

Women are certainly action oriented—they want what they want, and they usually get it. But they use a more subtle action—one found in relationship—than men use. I've made Jackie happiest not by *doing* something for her, but by *being* something. Being kind, patient, caring, or just an attentive listener when she shares something with me. She even thanks me for it! And I respond, "I didn't do anything. I just sat there and listened." She explains, "But it's *how* you listened." The man values life by doing, the woman by feeling.

Simon Baron-Cohen, a leading scholar on sex difference, outlines the primary contrasts between the female and male mind on the first page of his excellent book *The Essential Difference:* "The female brain is predominantly hard-wired for empathy. The male brain is predominantly hard-wired for understanding and building systems."[2]

The woman is more about relationship, care, and equity. This is true of different kinds of women from Margaret Thatcher and Eleanor Roosevelt to Julie Andrews and Sandra Bullock. The man is more about getting stuff done, delivering the goods, and conquering. This is true for different kinds of men from Joe Lieberman and Henry Ford to Jeff Gordon and Tony Dungy.

Boys don't have BFFs. They don't have the relational intensity that girls exhibit. You see this relational nature in women everywhere. In the beautiful city of Amsterdam recently, I sat in a café looking out on a busy boulevard and noticed that nearly everyone rides bikes to where they're going. Most do so alone, going to work, school, or the store. But sometimes you see larger groups of men and groups of women riding together. And the men surely like being together as they ride, but they typically ride head forward to get where they need to go. The women ride along to their destination, but they do so while chatting up a storm. For the women, the bike ride isn't merely a utilitarian task or a challenge as it is for the men. It's more of, "Let's have a nice time together while we are getting there." I saw it right in front of me.

Women connect at deeper levels when they've learned to work out the bumpy parts of relational intensity. This often happens in their middle school years. As parents, we need to be aware of this nature in our daughters and help them develop strong and stable relationships. We must even teach them to become trusted peacemakers and bridge builders among their less mature peers. This is the role of a confident and mature girl.

WOMEN ARE WISELY RECEPTIVE

As a woman draws those she values toward herself, she is also receptive. This is part of her physical and psychological orientation. But a mature and healthy woman never receives indiscriminately. The healthier she is in general, the healthier she is in her discernment. She chooses slowly and receives wisely. She doesn't receive everyone who wants her. This quality is very powerful, not because women are unfairly held to a higher standard than men, but because we subtly realize that for a woman, to be more selective is a virtue. And parents, particularly dads, help develop this confidence and wisdom in their girls.

Women are receptive in other ways as well, beyond the physical. I remember a simple piece of advice I read many years ago from a man who taught parents how to keep their children safe in an unsafe world. He encouraged parents to teach their children that if they ever got separated in a large store, an amusement park, or some other public area, to go to a "mom or grandma" and ask for help.

Why? First off, women in general are safer. More important, a woman who is a mother is the safest creature on earth! For a child who is lost, the very best place to be is with the nearest mother. She's highly likely to be safe, comforting, and doggedly determined to reconnect child with parent. She knows empathetically how the child's disconnected mother feels. Women are receptive.

Yet both moms and dads must make sure their daughters aren't blindly receptive. They must use good judgment in deciding who to let into their lives. It starts with the little abandoned cat in the neighborhood. Our daughters will tell us we just *have* to take the kitty and raise it as our own. In fact, they would have no problem turning the house into a menagerie, but it's our role to teach them that this is neither wise nor realistic.

A young woman needs to show this same judgment when receiving a young man into her life, as a possible husband and the potential father of her children. I tell my girls they are so precious to me that it will be nearly impossible for them to find a husband who will love and care for them nearly as much as I do. While I've made their social lives a bit more difficult, as their dad, I won't settle for anything less than what's best for them. They know I'm kidding, but they also find comfort in the truth that a good and dependable man is watching out for them. All girls need this, and it comes best from their dad.

WOMEN SEEK SECURITY

While men are chance takers, women are oriented toward being secure. The male's orientation is to go out and find a place within another to create his future. He must take a chance in finding this woman, knowing he could be rebuffed and rejected. Yet he must take this step. If he weren't wired for chance, he would become a human cul-de-sac, a road ending with himself and leading nowhere.

The woman's orientation is much different. Because she seeks security, she asks herself, *Will this man be safe? Will he be faithful? Will he care for, protect, and stick by me and our baby?* Her future, and their future together, depends heavily on this. The woman guided only by, "Oh, he was *so* handsome and seemed so interested in me," usually ends up disappointed if that romantic "handsome" and "interested in me" is not backed up by "dependable" and "trustworthy." This is a deeply instinctual dance for her, if she is secure: to choose wisely and then to receive and to nourish.

We can see this quality in a woman when she becomes pregnant. Once the news of the new life within is manifest, she won't stop thinking about the security, safety, and well-being of this new life for the rest of her life. This is a primary and powerful essence of womanhood, and the future of the human race depends on it. This relentless pursuit of security by our mothers is what brought and helped each of us to this very moment. Very few people are unaffected, whether negatively or positively, by the security choice their mom made in the man who would become their father.

Women Prefer Modesty

Women aren't as sexually aggressive or adventurous as men. They're more selective and reserved. This is cross-cultural. They typically demonstrate more modesty about their physicality.

Modesty is a basic *human* quality. We see it develop naturally in our children as they grow. But modesty is much more basic to women. At the gym or on a camping trip, men will more likely just change and shower in a locker room right out there for all to see. Many boys learned to deal with this in gym class—it's what guys do. But a woman isn't wired that way. Her modesty is the naturally driven desire to protect something very precious and valuable: the power of her femininity. Healthy women recognize the power of their femininity and use it in healthy ways. Unhealthy women don't.

One of the modern world's first scholars of sex was Havelock Ellis. He was among the most liberal thinkers of his day and beyond. His massive six-volume *Studies in the Psychology of Sex* begins with a discussion of modesty. Writing in the academic disjointed style of 1899, Ellis explains,

> Modesty, which may be provisionally defined as an almost
> instinctive fear prompting to concealment and usually centering
> around the sexual processes, while common to both sexes is more
> peculiarly feminine, so that it may almost be regarded as the chief
> secondary sexual character of women on the psychical side. The
> woman who is lacking in this kind of fear is lacking, also, in
> sexual attractiveness to the normal and average man.[3]

Mothers help build and protect this sense of modesty in girls, of course. But fathers again play a major role in helping girls construct a healthy sense of womanly modesty, which is curiously related to their sense of confidence. Just as we talked about what boys without good fathers do with their physical strength and power, the same is true of girls denied good fathers. The girl who doesn't have the power and beauty of her femininity affirmed by the first and most important man in her life will grow into a woman driven to flaunt it in the face of every young and older man, constantly making the very public and insecure statement, "I desperately need you to notice me as a woman!" Of course, the responses from the many males she does attract never fulfill but only make her feel emptier because it is more opportunistic than truly loving.

What Ellis said at the dawn of the last century is still true today. We see modesty as a womanly virtue because it encompasses the idea that this person matters deeply—not just as a human being, but as a very special sort of human. The quiet and confident knowledge that makes up a woman's femininity is very valuable and powerful indeed, perhaps the greatest human power that exists. It's the demand that she be treated with honor and respect by others, especially males. And this quality makes her especially interesting and desirable to good men. This is the message we need to teach our girls today.

WOMEN CARE

In his book *What Could He Be Thinking?* Michael Gurian includes a fun quiz[4] to find out how masculine or feminine you are. One of the questions is about what you'd do if you saw some kids playing a physical game and one fell to the ground after being hurt. The options are these:

(a) Yell, "Get up and shake it off!"

(b) Wait a few moments to see if the child is okay. If you sense he is, challenge him to get back into the fun.

(c) Move quickly to the child, bend down to see if she is okay, then help her to her feet.

Which do you think are the masculine and feminine answers?

Women are poised toward and more likely to offer aid and care. It wasn't a man who started the American Red Cross.

Of course, compassion isn't exclusive to women. Caring is a virtue of strength that should be taught to both boys and girls, while realizing that our girls have a more natural inclination toward it. When I'm playing at a park with our children, Gurian's question realizes itself. A child falls down hurt. I'm most likely to stand there and observe the child for a moment. But my girls yell at me, "Dad! Go over there and see if he's okay!" So I do. Our different reactions show our concern in different ways. They are more immediate and responsive. I want to see if the child can shake it off and get it together on his own. As a boy, I'd much rather have someone leave me alone and let me get myself together than to make a fuss over me.

Fathers must remember that our wives and daughters are likely to react more quickly to someone's pains and hurts. Just as our slower response isn't because we don't care, their immediate reaction isn't because they are nervous or anxious. Rather, their care is wired into their womanhood.

Women Use Words

I've heard that women have a need to say no fewer than ten thousand words in a day, while a man has a need to say only seven hundred fifty in a day. This factoid has been challenged recently, and I think for good reason. I do agree that women tend to use more words than men, but the spread isn't as large as some claim. However, what *is* distinct is what men and women talk about and how. Men tend to use words to communicate information or ideas. Women tend to use words to communicate feelings and thoughts and to gather them from others.

This concept is pretty easy to understand. Think about how the same word or phrase can have very different meanings depending on how it's said and when. You fix the copier at work, and someone says, "Aren't you the smart one?" and you feel good about it. But if you break the copier, the same words take on a much different meaning.

Now come back to the differing qualities of women and men. A phrase like, "Are you going to wear that?" is understood as a question to a man. But it's a statement to a woman—and not a helpful one. In the same way, when a wife asks her husband, "Would you like to do the dishes tonight?" the man hears it as a question. But it's actually meant by the woman as a request to do the dishes. Women tend to mean more by their words than men do.

Both mothers and fathers need to understand and appreciate this when communicating with their daughters, recognizing that because they mean more with their words, they can sometimes read more into your words than you intend. Mothers can help their daughters recognize and temper this tendency in themselves. In addition, fathers can learn to appreciate their daughters' more roundabout way, thus creating a warmer connection with them.

WOMEN DESIRE EQUITY AND SUBMISSION

This is a difficult feminine quality to talk about, because the issue has become emotionally charged and can easily be misunderstood. So I enter these waters with care, knowing that it's too important to ignore.

A woman doesn't want to be a sexual object or plaything. She's not. Rather, she's a person who loves and wants to be treated as a person by her lover. She's an equal, although a unique sort of equal. Different doesn't mean unequal. Are Haitians unequal to Swedes because they're different?

Men and women are equal in their humanity, but different in their abilities and qualities. This doesn't mean one is better than another overall, but they certainly excel in specific talents and abilities. Women don't have the body strength of men. Men don't have the intuitive sense that women have. These and plenty of other differences don't make male and female unequal; rather these differences make them necessary for each other.

In this light, it's not a weakness that women want to be led, protected, and cared for. In the sexual embrace, the most universal and comfortable position for both man and woman is what most of us call the missionary position. But anthropologists explain it has gone by many other names in its long, multicultural history: the matrimonial position, the mama-papa position, or the male-superior position. These names come from the way most men and women in various cultures choose to embrace and find most fulfilling. Men typically enjoy being the dominant or superior player here and women the submissive. It enhances a woman's feeling of being taken and swept up by her man. It's not a sign of weakness.

This submissive position and experience, consciously and freely entered into by most women, is enhanced all the more when the woman knows she is cared for, respected, and honored by her husband, rather than merely used. This is one reason researchers consistently report that married sex is more fulfilling and satisfying to both partners both physically and emotionally than nonmarital sex.[5] The woman can safely feel taken by her man because she knows he holds her lovingly as an equal and beautiful being. He is committed to her.

A few months ago, I was interviewed by a thirty-something single woman journalist from a fancy New York magazine. She was no Kansas girl. She was writing a story on single mothers and asked me about single women like her who choose to be single mothers. We were talking about whether most single moms want men in their lives. We both agreed that indeed they do. In fact, she told me that she would get married right after work that evening if she could find a good, responsible man.

I asked her what she wanted most in a man. Her answer actually surprised me. This confident and highly skilled woman said she wanted a man who would care for and provide for her, protect her, and make her feel safe. *That's what she said.* What she wanted most was a good man she could essentially submit herself to, not as a servant or doormat, but as a woman seeking security and care.

As I've interviewed many different kinds of women from diverse backgrounds for my research on this book, I asked, "What are you looking for most in a potential husband?" I was struck by how nearly every one of them answered, "Someone to care for me and feel secure with." I don't think any of these women were incapable of caring for themselves. These were statements not of need or inability but of desire.

This healthy submission can and should come from a place of strength in our daughters. In our family, we do this by telling and demonstrating to our girls that they're worth our care and protection. I try to open the car doors for my daughters not because they can't do it for themselves, but because I want to teach them to expect such respect from a man. They should feel secure submitting themselves to such help. And I tell my girls they cannot settle for a man who doesn't love them as much as I do. They find great security in knowing I would do anything for them. I will not tolerate any man in their lives who fails to treat them as well and as respectfully as I do. These men will get that message loud and clear.

This understanding of submission actually empowers women—something the New York journalist and the women I interviewed understand. As girls understand and expect this empowerment from submission, it will motivate their husbands—someone's sons—to become thoughtful, strong, and considerate men in order to please their wives.

Women Wield Soft Power, Which Shapes Humanity

Women wield remarkable power. You'll recall that men must be brave risk takers. Why brave? Because they risk being shot down by the women they are interested in.

Women really do call the shots here—or at least they could if they only would. Our hook-up, easy-sex culture is not based on the woman's terms. It's a meat market on the immature male's terms. Unfortunately, women are surrendering their power and influence to opportunistic and weak boys. Talk about unhealthy and demeaning submission. Why do so many smart young women subject themselves to this today? And they constantly report how unfulfilling it is for them.[6]

Women actually hold most of the power in a marriage, and they wield it best from a position of gentle confidence. The first human males got up and started hunting and gathering food for their families because the women expected it and communicated their expectations to these men. Consider that manners exist because women exist.

Women have always demonstrated power and influence. They show this power in a hundred ways, such as controlling the access of the man to his children. Or they motivate their husbands simply by communicating their disapproval over a certain behavior. These facts explain in part why marriage is a sexual and domestic relationship on the woman's terms and cohabitation is a sexual and domestic relationship on the man's terms.

And this ability to wield power and influence is true not only of women but of young girls too. I experienced this in my own boyhood. I remember a girl in my sixth-grade class. Susan very much had my attention. She was blond, pretty, confident, and smart. Another boy, Eric, was pushing me around verbally, and I caved easily to his threats. In front of everyone, Susan asked me, "Why do you let that ape push you around?"

My first reaction was embarrassment and mortification. My second was "duh"—couldn't she see that Eric was huge and would pound me? But of course, I realize now, as every man does, that I would have had much less trouble with Eric and his ilk if I had looked him confidently in the eyes, squinted just a bit for effect, and said in a very low, slow, and commanding tone, "Listen. I really don't think you want to mess with me. You don't know how out of control I can get!" and just left it at that.

But Susan's rebuke stayed with me for all these years, and it reminds me even today at age forty-eight, "Stand up for yourself! Don't let people bully you." Susan's confident challenge prompted me to different actions from that moment on. She unknowingly helped me along the road to manhood that day in sixth grade. And she has no idea. No small thing indeed!

Consider how William Golding's classic novel *Lord of the Flies* would have turned out differently had there been just one young woman on the island with all those boys. Who can doubt that the mere presence of a female would have had a profound impact on the boys' choices because of their interest in pleasing her and winning her attention?

Girls do help shape boys with their expectations. This is such a primary part of the power of women, yet so few recognize it. We are wise parents to help our girls realize the power they possess in femininity and how a good woman uses this power without even seeming like she is. Soft and quiet power is the most influential sort.

WOMEN ARE ABOUT CONNECTING

I saved one of the most obvious feminine qualities for last. This quality is clear when it comes to sex. For the man, sex is largely about the sex. For the woman, sex is more about connecting.

Women seek connection in their sexuality not because women are more sentimental and romantic than men, but because it's how their female bodies and souls are oriented. When a woman engages with a man, there's a very real possibility of her becoming a mother. (Remember, birth control is a relatively new development in the sexual playing field.) Given this, her body and her whole womanly essence is geared toward connecting and bonding with this man who could very possibly become the father of her new child. If a mother is anything, she's all about making sure her baby has what is needed to be healthy, safe, secure, and happy. The woman knows this man will be her child's first and most important resource—after herself, of course. So her instinctual nature is to connect and bond well with her lover.

Of course, all of this doesn't consciously go through every woman's mind as she considers a sexual mate, because it runs deeper through the soul and wiring of a woman. That's why it's rarer and more difficult for a woman to casually approach a sexual connection with a man. It goes against her very nature. And when she does, she is more likely to be more unfulfilled than the man. In fact, all societies have used marriage to regulate sexuality and to make sure this attachment between potential mother and father is established before the chance of babies is possible. With the decline of marriage and the increase of fatherlessness, we shouldn't be surprised to see what sociologists call the "feminization of poverty," driven by the rise in single motherhood.

However, this connecting quality isn't confined just to sexuality and potential mothering. The woman is wired to connect at many levels, even with her friends. Of course, we have to teach our girls to keep these relationships in perspective and not get too intense about who is spending time with whom and whether it's all fair. As noted earlier, this relational focus starts to intensify among girls in the fifth and sixth grades. Our girls should learn that their confidence and self-esteem don't come from their relationships. These relationships should be a great source of joy and happiness in their lives, not a source of conflict. Connecting is important for girls, but it can't rule them.

As our girls grow, they should come to expect that the men in their lives can learn how to connect well also. Their serious boyfriends should certainly be young men who are developing some ability at connecting. It's never a valid excuse for a man to claim, "I'm just not relational. I have a hard time getting close to people and letting them in." This statement might be true, but he must learn how to do this in order to be truly human.

Your Amazing Girl

Our girls, and the women they become, are more likely to:
- be confidently enticing
- value intimacy over action
- be receptive
- seek security
- be modest
- be caring
- relate with words
- seek equity and submission
- wield soft power that shapes humanity
- connect to others

As the parent of a daughter, your job is to pay close attention to the kind of girl God has given you and raise her toward womanhood with the qualities we've discussed. Of course, you'll need to consider which of these qualities you need to nurture or temper, realizing these either are or are not a strong part of your own daughter's makeup.

Just like boys entering the world of manhood, girls need a guide into this amazing, mysterious, and beautiful world of authentic womanhood. And that journey will look a little different for every girl. And a mother and father are both necessary guides in different ways along this path.

———

My husband and I have two daughters and one son. The girls are the oldest, three years apart. Our second daughter seems to have no interest in anything girly. Should this be of concern to us? If so, what should we be concerned about?

This is a relatively common question. You shouldn't necessarily be concerned. Does she seem comfortable being a girl, even if it's in her own way? Girls might be more boyish—that is, enjoy more boy-typical activities—but do them very well as girls.

We have a girl in our neighborhood who you'd never find wearing a dress; jeans and T-shirt are her standard issue. She has no interest in dolls or typical girl games. She's a textbook tomboy. But she's clearly very comfortable being a girl. She has beautiful, wavy long hair that she sometimes tucks under a baseball cap. She wears little stud pierced earrings. She's also very sensitive to knowing if other kids are being treated fairly when playing. She's a healthy little girl, just different.

Girls like this, who are clearly comfortable being a different kind of girl but a girl all the same, don't trouble me. Girls who seem overly fixated on doing boy things in boy ways are more of a concern, especially when they seem fixated on hiding any hint of their feminine design. We should all be comfortable being who we are.

I do think you can help your daughter find feminine things she feels comfortable identifying with. These connections might not seem big in themselves, but they can help her make subtle but important identifications with her femininity. A good example is the earrings our neighborhood girl wears. They're clearly feminine, but not overly so. I trust her mom or dad has lightly encouraged her to wear them, probably by commenting on how nice they look. This helps her connect with her womanhood without feeling shoved into a "girly girl" box, which wouldn't be helpful for her.

The primary key is to listen to and closely read your daughter and try to see where her strengths and struggles are. Encourage her sex-distinct strengths, and gently address her struggles by directing her (in ways that seem natural for her) toward the qualities discussed in this chapter.

You talked about girls having the power to shape and mold boys and men. Why should that be their responsibility?

My first reaction is to say, "No, it's not their responsibility; it's their privilege," because it somehow makes the task more enticing. However, it is their responsibility. Not as individuals but in a collective sense.

Gail Collins is the editorial page editor of the *New York Times,* no female traditionalist to be sure. A few years ago, she wrote a book titled *America's Women,* a wonderful history of the role everyday women played in the founding of our nation. When she was interviewed on National Public Radio about her book, the interviewer asked, "What's the most important role women have played in the founding and success of our country?"

She didn't hesitate a moment, startling the interviewer (and many listeners, no doubt, including me) with this statement: "To make men behave." Collins explained that from the founding of the colonies to the engine that drove the Industrial Revolution, women got men to apply themselves and get down to work to overcome the next hurdle and produce whatever was needed next. In fact, this is true of most cultures—at least monogamous ones. Women really do wield the soft power to shape men into cultured and productive beings.

Q Do you think parents should encourage girls to pursue nontraditional female careers?

A The primary goal in pointing both boys and girls toward professions is to pay close attention to the giftings and interests of your children and to give them ideas of work they can do that utilizes those talents.

I do think it is important to let our girls know the opportunities are wide open for them, regarding what they want to do in life. Of course, young children will pick a rash of different career goals. One of our daughters wants to be a singer, a nurse, a "horse rider," and a truck driver. No doubt some or all of these passions will fade away in the years to come. But we should encourage our children even in the unlikely things. Amelia Earhart was in a man's world, but she was very much a woman there.

Also, it's important to note that the Scriptures don't give a great deal of guidance or mandates on the work men and women should or should not do by sex distinction. Read Genesis 1:28–29, which outlines God's command for what man and woman should do as workers, inhabitants of the world, builders of human culture, and custodians of the plants and animals. Make note of the jobs God gives to man and the ones He gives to woman.*

---

* Don't strain yourself trying to find God's separate jobs for man and woman. They're not there. God gave these jobs for man and woman to do together, and prior to the Industrial Revolution, most husbands and wives worked together in the primary livelihood that supported their family unit. This is where we derived certain last names like the Coopers, the Smiths, the Hunters, the Merchants; they stem from the family's principal craft or trade. Only with the arrival of the Industrial Revolution did men and women start working separately, doing different jobs alongside other people's husbands and wives in factories, offices, department stores, and so on.

THREE

What a Boy
Needs Most

A few years ago, I was speaking on gender differences at a northeastern university. After my presentation, a thoughtful and polite student approached me. He told me that my comments about the larger differences in male and female not being cultural were clearly mistaken. He then proceeded to inform me that only recently in human experience have men and women started to act and dress differently. I listened carefully with interest to see how he would explain this to me.

He must have been a fashion-design student, because he went into great detail explaining how men's and women's distinct fashions were relatively new. He said that for most of history, men and women dressed essentially the same and that gender distinction in clothing didn't exist. I was impressed that he at least tried to support his assertions with specific details rather than just declaring his position to be "fact," as many students do.

As he finished, I asked if he was a student of the fine arts, particularly sculpture and painting. He indicated he was, so I asked him if it wasn't true that you could pick art from any human epoch and culture and have no real difficulty distinguishing the men in the images from the women, even if their style of dress was very different from ours today and if you had no knowledge of their culture. A classic and unmistakable "now, that's an interesting point my professors never told me about!" look came over his face. I let him down easily, agreeing that men's and women's dress does differ from culture to culture and time to time, but still, we don't have any problem noticing differences in gender.

Sex and gender difference is natural, deeply rooted, and very real, both in ourselves and in human culture. It's how we know ourselves and how we know others. From this truth, we can teach our children what boys are. Notice that I intentionally said that we can teach our *children* what boys are, not just teach our *boys* what boys are. Let me explain.

Boys certainly need to learn what boys are, because their destiny is a healthy boyhood that leads to healthy manhood. But boys are also a key part of our girls' destinies. So girls must understand what a healthy boy is and how those qualities lead to a good man. In addition, boys and girls learn a great bit about themselves by understanding the nature and qualities of their opposite. Try to explain "cold" to someone who has no understanding of "hot."

Learning what a boy is constitutes an important life lesson. But many of us were raised without even really thinking about it much—or so it seemed. The truth is that we were thinking about it all the time. We just didn't take much notice about what a boy is—or what a girl is, and the differences between the two—because it just seemed so natural.

Of course, not everyone accepts that these larger gender differences are natural. Consider the gender-neutral enthusiasts who want us to buy into their idea that, beyond genitalia and reproduction, the differences between male and female are artificial, cultural constructs used only for shoving people into boxes so they can be controlled and manipulated. Harvard professor Harvey Mansfield wisely counters this illusion, explaining there are no genuinely gender-neutral human beings anywhere in the world. In fact, he says gender neutrality is a cultural construct: "The gender-neutral society cannot simply let nature take its course.... Pressure in favor of gender neutrality needs to be applied."[1] Surely, if gender differences were artificial, we'd have examples of cultures where males and females are indistinguishable. We would find examples of interesting and unique creatures that couldn't be labeled male or female. But this doesn't happen.

Everyone can be distinguished sexwise by either overt or subtle indicators. This is true not just in their physicality but in their spirit, essence, and manner of being. If this weren't true, a statement like, "Hey, he runs like a girl" would be nonsense, similar to, "Hey, he runs like a real-estate appraiser!" Or the bit in an old *Seinfeld* episode about one of Jerry's dates who had "man hands" wouldn't be funny; the humor is in the premise that we all agree on what a typical woman's hands look like.

Gender distinction and appreciation is natural and organic, and we find it happening in all cultures, everywhere, throughout time.

As a parent raising a boy, it is your job to become a student of what is naturally mannish or boylike in the subtle ways masculinity shows itself, so you can help develop such qualities in your boy according to his temperament and style.

About a Boy

The first thing to know for sure about a boy is this: *a boy is a young male on his way to manhood.* If you forget everything else you learn about males, this singular truth will take you far. This is really the center of the bull's-eye for raising boys. If you're raising a boy, the objective is healthy manhood. Everything else falls in place behind this truth.

Gather a group of twenty- and thirty-something women, married or not, and ask them if healthy and vibrant manhood is an important destination for parents in raising boys or whether it doesn't really matter. They will have a very definite response—not because they are traditionalists or know what parenting is all about but because they see a definite shortage of real men their age today. Instead, they are finding far too many boys who have aged chronologically but haven't progressed much past their joystick-obsessed, porn-watching, prank-playing, beer-soaked teen years. Of course, this isn't true of all male young adults, but it's too true of far too many.

A culture of good manhood is shaped, or not, by parents. No other part of a society is in the business of making men, not even the marines. They can only make men out of young men who are already moving well in that direction.

Mamas, don't let your babies grow up to be boy-men!

Boys in God's Image

The second thing to know for sure about a boy is his creation. Remember in the very first chapter of Scripture, God makes two very profound statements. First, God declares, "Let Us make man in Our image, according to Our likeness" (Genesis 1:26). Here God announces His intention to create something that reflects, shows, and demonstrates His very image and likeness. This creation will be a visible, earthly picture of the invisible, divine God.

In the next verse, God reveals this unique creation: "So God created man in His own image; in the image of God He created him; male and female He created them" (verse 27).

Wow! This creation that bears the very image of God, this earthly picture of God, is the human being as male and female. And the boy you are raising is one of these amazing one-of-a-kind male God-pictures in the flesh. Think about that! You're raising a particular kind of God-imager, one called "boy."

Call your boy right now, or when you see him next, and just ask him to stand in front of you for a few moments. *Behold him!* This creature is one of the most amazing beings in the universe. I'm serious. God tells us so! Mysteriously, this boy of yours in his masculinity is God's message to you and the whole world of what God's own image and likeness is. Now explain to your boy that he is God's image. Tell him how special he is, not just as a human, but as a *male* human. God explains this difference in the verse we just read, and He does so because the male-female distinction is fundamental to our God-imaging purpose. We don't know *how* exactly, but we know it is, because God said so.

Both our boys and our girls need to learn this amazing and beautiful truth, because it will change everything about how they see and understand themselves and others. It will also change how you as the parent of a boy—charged and trusted with the task of bringing him into this thing call manhood—do your job. You can't simply dismiss a male God-imager. The same holds true about female God-imagers, which we'll discuss in the following chapter.

With that, let's look at some of the things that make boys on the road to manhood distinct and fascinating creatures. What is it that a boy needs to know about himself in getting him onto and moving along the man road? What does he need to complete his mission to manhood? And as the parent of your remarkable boy, how can you nudge him along the way?

Boys Yearn to Make a Difference

All of us need to know we're needed—that we're important to someone and valuable to our community. But something within a boy causes this value and sense of importance to come not so much from what he is or who he has as friends but from what he *does*. A boy needs to know that what he does can make a difference and that he has the goods, the talents, and strengths to make a difference. Men continually search for significance through work and skill, and they are crushed if they don't find it.

The need to make a difference explains why men are more likely to assume leadership roles. Men don't desire to lead as some kind of subversive plot against women. In fact, their leadership is a plot *for* women, acting out their natures to lead, provide, and protect. Men lead because the male's orientation is to shape, mold, create, and change things that are bad into something good.

Picture someone who is described as a "workaholic." How often do you hear a woman described that way? Certainly, women aren't lazy. In fact, most women are delirious multitaskers who handle a great deal of income earning and home care within families. Women do what needs to be done, but they aren't as likely as men to push the limits beyond what needs doing in order to affirm themselves.

Workaholics are less secure in themselves in certain ways and so work to make themselves feel significant. I deal with this myself. I tell those I confide in that I work so hard because I feel as if I need to justify the space I'm taking up in the world. Yes, that's an unhealthy way to view myself, but it was deeply drilled into me in some way in childhood and is difficult to shake.

Look at the typical boy's heroes. Beyond the fictional superheroes, many boys admire baseball, football, or soccer players who make the impossible game-winning score or acrobatic save in the last few seconds of the match. The boy wants to be that man—so much that he will imagine being his hero, practicing for hours so he can run, kick, throw, or swing a bat like his hero. The guy who "just gets by" is seldom a hero. The boy's hero is usually more about ability than character!

Measuring up, meeting expectations, and getting approval are important to both our sons and our daughters. But making a difference is a far bigger and essential deal for our boys. They need it like oxygen. If they don't get approval for the ways they are important, primarily from dad, they'll be ruled by the pursuit of significance the rest of their lives—usually in unhealthy and sometimes manipulative ways.

What to Teach Your Boy About Making a Difference

Give your son age-appropriate challenges. Boys might not like it, but they need to be pushed. This allows them to learn what it means to take reasonable chances and succeed by hard work and applying themselves. As they grow older, make the chances and challenges a little tougher so your boy stretches and pushes himself.

When your son meets the goal, be sure to praise him. But the important balance is to make sure he doesn't attempt things too difficult, at the danger of breaking his spirit by always failing. However, as noted earlier, a boy doesn't always have to "win" to gain confidence. In fact, boys learn confidence and fulfillment by making progress—doing better this week or month and having someone notice. Your son should learn that progress, even by the most modest measures, is the prize.

Also, praise your boy for what you see him doing: helping around the house, showing kindness to others, performing in music or sports, or even expressing a creative idea. Let him know you are watching and are impressed.

I was twenty-one before my father ever told me that one of my ideas influenced him. When I was growing up, he would tell me I was good at sports, his thing. But he would never praise me for thoughts and ideas, my thing. I don't think he meant to withhold such affirmation from me. He just wasn't aware of how important ideas were to me and how much I needed his affirmation in this area. Dad, don't make the same mistake with your boy. Be sure not to praise him only for what matters to you, but look for and appreciate what matters to him, even if it's far afield from your interests. In fact, rejoice that God has given you this wonderful, unique little individual.

Our boys need their thing to be our thing. We need to be generous and sincere in our encouragement and praise of what they go after. Sometimes we even need to point out to them the real difference they are making and how consequential that is. Help them see what they can't always see for themselves.

BOYS NEED TO SAVE THE WORLD

In addition to making a difference, boys need a big mission. Boys want to and need to think big—both in saving those who need help and also in the fullness of the world, and sometimes in galaxies far, far away.

Jim Collins, the world-famous business and management writer, explains in *Good to Great* that every successful company or organization requires what he calls a BHAG—a Big Hairy Audacious Goal. A BHAG is so big, ambitious, and daring that it seems crazy to even consider it. This kind of challenge excites boys and men. It's precisely why I want to help our society understand the fundamental natures and importance of authentic masculinity and femininity. Something within the male drives him to set his sights on something big, hairy, and audacious.

Typically, it's a boy who stands on the beach and watches the ships go over the horizon or huge jetliners streak across the sky. He wonders where they're going, what dangers they might face along the way, and how they will overcome them. And he wants to be a man on that ship or plane one day and have the adventures they are having.

Girls don't think so much about going to the moon or Mars. Sure, Dora the Explorer goes on plenty of adventures, but she can't go without her good friends Map and Backpack. Men typically want to go it alone. The great explorers in history are men, and it's not necessarily because women who wanted the jobs were pushed aside. Rather, the men had the passion to launch out, not knowing if success or death awaited them. But go they did. The American Civil War, the Normandy landings on D-day, the *Apollo 11* moon landing, and the exploits of the Vikings are riveting to boys because the men involved took great risks with huge and historic payoffs.

What to Teach Your Boy About Saving the World

Parents need to work together to give their sons the room to go out and reform their world. Don't be afraid to place challenges before your son. Even though you are tasked with keeping your boy safe from harm and you worry about his being crushed by failed attempts, you must push him appropriately, because challenges build confidence, strength, and wisdom.

Tell your son about Abraham Lincoln, who lost more elections than he won, and how his final election battle made such a difference. Tell him about Thomas Edison, who never gave up after so many failures and how life is so much better, safer, and enjoyable today because of his perseverance.

Perseverance is the lesson our boys must learn in working to save the world. For our boys, anything worth doing is going to be a difficult challenge.

BOYS NEED TO DESTROY THE WORLD

While boys are brave rescuers, they're also inclined to destroy, for purposes both good and bad. Something within a boy compels him to break and smash things. If he can break and smash things while rescuing someone, all the better. This is why "fireman," "army man," and "policeman" are hugely popular answers to the "What do you want to be when you grow up, son?" question. These guys get to bust stuff, save people, *and* get paid for it! What's cooler than that?

Boys like to take things apart, even things that are supposed to stay together, just for the sake of reducing them to their most basic parts. My son, Schaeffer, has a treasure box where he keeps all kinds of interesting items, such as foreign coins left over from my trips and bottle caps I've given him. But he also saves little parts of things: a dissected watch, the base of a broken light bulb, a broken cell phone, or a gear or module of some sort. These items aren't junk or they wouldn't be in his *treasure* box. He loves to break things down and bury them in his box, like a dog with a bone. Anyone but a boy would call it a junk box. But to a boy, it's a treasure.

Consider also that boys are more attracted to fire than girls are. Boys like fire because it destroys and consumes things in some mysterious way. In the movie *The School of Rock,* the teacher (played by Jack Black) asks Freddy Jones, a slacker slumped down in the back of the class, what he likes to do when he's not in school. Freddy answers flatly, "I dunno… burn stuff." Classic boy!

Boys also love monster trucks because monster trucks smash and crush regular trucks. The destroy-the-world factor explains why boys are also more attracted to fireworks, guns, army men, and explosives.

What to Teach Your Boy About Destroying the World

Dad needs to show his son how to destroy the right things safely. And mom needs to let him. Dad also needs to show his boy how much fun it can be to destroy certain things. Through this, the boy comes to the important realization that, "Hey, my dad has the urge to burn, blow up, and destroy stuff just like I do." This makes the boy feel a part of something rather than just weird. But when dad takes certain precautions before he destroys, his son will learn where the boundaries are.

BOYS NEED TO KNOW THEY ARE SMART

Boys not only want to be strong, they also want to be brilliant. Yet many boys have difficulty achieving grades that reflect their intelligence, so they need support and encouragement in other ways. Our boys need to know that book and school smarts are important, but so are other kinds of smarts: people smarts, negotiating smarts, debating and arguing smarts, mechanical smarts, survival smarts, even trivia smarts.

I read books incessantly because of an internal sense that I'm always on the lowest level of the smartest-guy-in-the-room quotient. So I read to learn. I'm never really satisfied. Most men are driven by some sense of personal inadequacy, and often their greatest successes derive from this. Other men want to know everything they can about a topic, be it working on cars, baseball trivia, hunting, rock climbing, or electronics.

Your boy desperately needs to know that he has what it takes in the development and strengthening of his most powerful muscle, his brain.

What to Teach Your Boy About Being Smart

Your son must learn that a lot of different kinds of smarts can make him just as capable and skilled as book-smart boys. Your boy might not know the entire periodic table of the elements, but maybe he can rope a calf or dismantle and clean a rifle. He might not know how to change the oil in the lawn mower, but he knows more about Greek history or astronomy than anyone in his school.

Smart comes in all kinds of sizes, shapes, and colors, and your son should understand what kind of smarts God has gifted him with. Both mom and dad should help him realize this and affirm his areas of interest in their own ways.

Boys Need to See Their Bodies Developing Well

Both boys and girls are very aware of their bodies. While we might think girls are more interested in their appearance, boys—starting at the age of about eleven to thirteen—will start to look at themselves in the mirror. When your son looks at his reflection, he'll either gain confidence from seeing his body develop, his chest take its masculine shape, his shoulders broaden, and his face fill out, or he'll be anxious about what isn't taking place. Boys are waiting to see themselves develop "south of the border" as well.

When I was a Boy Scout, in about the sixth grade, I remember seeing an older boy, age seventeen or so, change after we all swam in the lake. I was shocked! I quietly felt sorry for him because he was way different down there than I was. Of course, I later found out I was the different one. Also, I developed more slowly than other boys, or at least I thought so at the time, and this made me scared of changing with my classmates in the locker room. I didn't want the other guys to know I was still a "boy." This was one of the most petrifying aspects of my early teen years.

Of course, it didn't take long for those changes to come, and I began to feel like one of the normal guys. In my late teens or so, I realized I'd been a normal boy all along and it wasn't really any big deal. Of course, at the time, it was the biggest deal in the world, and telling me that things would come along in time would have done little to ease my anxiety.

Your boy will face similar challenges, concerns, and hopes—whether he develops early, late, or right on time. And even if it doesn't seem to concern him, he needs to know that nature takes care of every boy eventually.

What to Teach Your Boy About His Developing Body

Parents can make "incidental" observations of their pre- and early-teen boys. Dad needs to say, "Wow, son. Your handshake is getting firm. Make sure not to crush someone's hand with that weapon!" Mom can ask if he needs new shirts "since your chest and shoulders are obviously getting broader." Comments like these accomplish exactly what your son wants: for you to make a big deal about his changing body without making a big deal about his changing body.

You also need to let your boy know what hormonal changes and urges to expect as his body changes, because those will come like a freight train. Your son's sexual drive will probably be like a mighty lion, and he needs to understand what it's for. Remind him that it's a gift from God and that it will also be his gift to his wife one day. Therefore, he should know healthy ways to care for and protect it.

Many boys are interested in helping build their bodies through workouts and weightlifting. Dad, you can help your son do this properly, safely, and with the discipline of endurance and consistency. If your son is interested, get with him. Let him be able to teach you some things rather than your doing all the teaching. Help him learn the difference between what's normal and natural in building muscle and what's obsessive and over the top.

Boys Need to Be Innovative

Boys want to build things from the ground up. You can see this in their play when imitating their heroes. Think of Kwai Chang Caine (played by David Carradine) on *Kung Fu,* who was so cool to boys my age. He could fight off anyone. Or MacGyver, the men of *The A-Team,* or Chuck Norris, whom many of today's dads wanted to be when they were boys. These guys could get themselves or others out of any situation with the materials at hand.

Today, boys young and old like to watch Bear Grylls on *Man vs. Wild.* This guy gets dropped from a helicopter into some desolate and extremely inhospitable wilderness situation with nothing but his clothing, maybe a jacket, and his knife. He has to survive for days as he finds his way back to civilization without the help of a compass. He is nothing but inventive. He can make insect repellent or toothpaste from tree bark. He knows what's edible and what's not in any geography. On one episode, he roasted and ate a scorpion and skinned a giant frog and ate it right there as a snack—no need to cook it! Guys watch this and realize they might not actually enjoy doing such things. But they wish they had the guts and innovation to do it.

For boys, this innovation has to do with independence, knowing they can do what they need to do without anyone's help. Sure, we all like the idea that we can push a few buttons on a phone and a pizza miraculously arrives at our house in thirty minutes or less. At the same time, we'd also like to be able to make pizza for ourselves when exiled five hundred miles from any other person.

What to Teach Your Boy About Being Innovative

High on the list of the greatest attributes of a good man are independence and self-sufficiency. Help your boy learn this in various situations.

Both mom and dad can ask your son how he would think himself out of a particular scenario. Make him take a good shot at solving the problem or situation on his own. "Your car goes off the road late one night and plunges into an icy lake and is sinking slowly. What do you do?" Give your son hints to help him discover the answer for himself.

Find books and Web sites that show these problem-solving and survival skills, and help your son put these new skills to practice. He should know how to start a fire without matches in at least two different ways with different materials. Challenge him to fix his own bike or to build a go-cart.

Your son wants to be a problem solver, and his wife will want him to be one. The main drive he needs—and it comes from *doing*—is to have the confidence to know he can figure nearly anything out if he has to.

BOYS NEED A SENSE OF DISCIPLINE

Contrary to popular opinion, most boys don't want to be slackers. They want adventure and excitement. They want to be able to deliver. They want to be excellent. The most important quality they need for each of these is discipline. Discipline means knowing the right thing to do and the right time to do it.

Anthropologists tell us that the primary problem in every human community throughout time and place is always the same: the unattached, undisciplined male. His male nature—with its raw physical strength and energies, appetites for food, drink, and sex, and even violence—needs to be domesticated and socialized. This doesn't mean men need to learn how to drink tea with their pinkie fingers sticking out. But they do need to learn how to live peaceably and productively with others while still being the men they, their family, and their community need them to be.

A good boy and man is one who knows how to discipline—which

literally means "to bridle"—the powerful horse or ox within him in useful and productive ways. This goes for his anger, strength, aggression, words, and sexuality. The male who is able to do so is a true man, no matter his age. The man who is unable or unwilling is not a true man, no matter his age. Bullies, who come in all ages, don't know anything about discipline. Men, on the other hand, are powerful, well-bridled beings.

What to Teach Your Boy About Discipline

Your son must learn that he is powerful in many ways. This power can be either good or bad, depending on how it's used. Discipline is the practice of using these powers in the proper ways for the right ends.

When you watch television shows or movies with your son or when you read books together, point out to him how the male characters either succeed or fail at showing discipline. The two different coaches in the final tournament in the movie *The Karate Kid* provide a great example. One wanted to be honorable, while the other wanted to win at any cost. Talk with your son about the consequences of both. How could the undisciplined man have shown more manly or gentlemanly behavior?

Discipline can be a struggle for parents because mom's sense of discipline will be different from dad's. Mom might think a boy demonstrating good self-discipline will never fight. Dad will be more inclined to teach the discipline of avoiding fights as much as possible, shutting a bully down with words or ignoring him. But then dad will say, "If push comes to shove, here's how you protect and stand up for yourself." A dad will teach a boy to send the message that he's not someone to be messed with. If fighting is necessary, he should do so without seriously or needlessly hurting his opponent. There's virtue in defending yourself from a bully who won't let up, but there's no virtue in pounding someone beyond what's called for. This is discipline, and it's what men do.

As you discuss discipline with your boy regularly, he is learning not only what is right, but also that "right" is important and worth studying. He'll learn to start doing this on his own, and it will teach him a great deal. His own discipline will help him lead and influence other boys for good. Discipline needs to come out in your son's relationships with others, because people are more important than anything else.

Boys Need to Have Good Called Out of Them

Related to discipline is the deep need in a boy to have the goodness within him called out. This is almost solely done by one or more men in the boy's circle. I say "almost solely" because women and girls can do this. Wives actually do it quite often for their men as they grow, mature, and age.

But as boys are growing up, having their goodness called out is largely and most powerfully done by men. As Margaret Mead observed, "Women, it is true, make human beings. But only men can make men."[2] I think that's one reason why millions of men were attracted to Promise Keepers in its heyday. These men called other men to be what men should be. It encouraged men—out of their common brokenness, vulnerability, and humility—to serve and honor others, particularly their wives and children. Much more than a pep talk or motivational event, Promise Keepers meetings represented a serious call and challenge. Men responded to it in significant ways.

Men like to be challenged by other men. This explains why a tough coach or teacher will become a deeply cherished life player in a boy's heart and soul. The key is having toughness, high expectations, and excellence paired with someone who loves and cares deeply. Boys need and value being pushed to accomplish the significant good that they hope lies within them. They need someone to call out the gifts, talents, and passions that God has placed within them.

What to Teach Your Boy About the Good in Him

Good men serve others in strong ways. Your boy has that vein of gold within, and he needs his mother and father and extended family to call it out of him. The good that lies within him is multilayered and is applied to those around him and to himself in his spiritual, intellectual, physical, and community life.

What unique good has God placed into your boy that needs to be called out of him, recognized, appreciated, and put to good use? Be sure to find it and call it out. Is your son a problem solver? Encourage him to put that talent to work with others, helping them get unstuck. Is he a champion of the underdog? Support his efforts to protect the weak and needy. Is your boy creative or athletic? Help him understand that his gift is not just about himself but for the benefit of others also.

Your son needs your help to recognize the good in himself if he is to become a good man.

BOYS NEED TO BE HONORABLE

The early church father John Chrysostom, speaking of the creatures in God's creation, said, "The bee is more honored than other animals, not because she labors, but because she labors for others." He uses the lowly but busy bee to teach us that to be honorable means to place ourselves in the service of others. Men need to serve others from a position of strength and ability, not weakness or timidity.

Think of places where men are often forged: the military, the police force, fire departments, high school and college football teams, the Boy

Scouts. In all of these places, honor is seen as central to a man's formation. Boys aspire to honor. Honor is a code that exists within the man, and therefore he has no real need for external controls or rules forced upon him. The honorable man is self-governed, and he can be trusted to do what is right.

My boss, Jim Daly, the president and CEO of Focus on the Family, tells the story of his wife, Jean, standing in the checkout aisle at the grocery store. One of their little guys was begging for some candy, and mom said, "No, not today." He responded by yelling at her.

The man waiting in line behind them saw the whole event. He stepped up and said, "Son, that's your mother, and it's not right for you to talk to her that way. You should always respect your mother! Understand?"

The boy was wide eyed, and Jean was thankful to have this man's support. He also happened to be an air force officer in uniform, which no doubt helped to increase the impact upon the boy. When Jean told Jim of the incident later that day, he was thankful for such a man correcting his son—glad there was another man in the community showing concern for both his son and his wife. This is honor by service.

What to Teach Your Boy About Being Honorable

Dad, you are the prime teacher here, both by example and expectations. My brother-in-law raised two big, tough boys, but he raised them to be gracious, honorable men. They were taught to allow the women to go first, to open a door for them as they did. If a meal was being prepared or someone needed help carrying the groceries, these boys were encouraged to jump in and ask how they could help. They were taught to say "yes sir" and "yes ma'am."

Our boys don't need to be taught that being honorable is better than being dishonorable. They get that. But they do need to be taught *how* to be honorable by the living examples of the men in their lives. When those men fail, as they surely will, they take responsibility and own up. Being honorable is making sure those around you who are stronger act as they should while taking care of and protecting those around you who are weaker.

Boys Need to Be Accepted and Respected by Peers and Elders

We know that girls tend to be more relational and boys more independent. But boys have a deep need to be respected by other boys and men. They do this by excelling at what the men around them are doing.

The need to be respected and accepted by peers and elders is why manhood initiation ceremonies are so important. While these are new to some communities, initiation lies behind the ancient idea of the Jewish bar mitzvah. This is a specific time and event where a boy is ushered by ceremony into the world of men. From here on, the young man is a different person. He's no longer a boy. He's expected to put childish things behind him and to move into the role of a man.

This acceptance and "calling up" of our boys is important. Many faith communities practice various forms of initiation ceremonies that are meaningful in ushering a boy from boyhood to manhood emotionally, spiritually, and physically. Look for those that help both father and son realize that both are accountable to God. Be wary of those that get fancy with all kinds of angles, props, emotionalism, and even spiritualism. The best are the simple, honest ceremonies where something meaningful is spoken into the boy by his father and other men, where something is expected from him, and where he is challenged. You can ask your pastor and youth pastor if they are aware of such ceremonies from your faith tradition.

What to Teach Your Boy About Being Accepting and Respectful

The first thing our boys need to learn is that respect not earned is meaningless. Respect is earned not by our skill or mastery of something but by our hustle, muscle, and sweat at *trying* to master something. All boys are looking for this respect and acceptance. Older peers and the men in their lives need to make them work just a bit for it but then reward them when they do.

Beyond earning respect and acceptance for themselves, our boys need to learn to accept and give respect to others when they've earned it. Good men and boys notice, honor, and praise the efforts of others.

THE DESIRES OF HIS HEART

Because they are men at heart, our sons already desire to possess and exhibit their masculinity. What are the things they desire?

- Boys yearn to make a difference.
- Boys need to save the world.
- Boys need to destroy the world.
- Boys need to know they are smart.
- Boys need to see their bodies developing.
- Boys need to be innovative.
- Boys need a sense of discipline.
- Boys need to have the good called out of them.
- Boys need to be honorable.
- Boys need to be accepted and respected by peers and elders.

Of course, these aren't the only things we need to teach our children about boys. You and your spouse can likely come up with other important male qualities that specifically match the nature, character, and personality of your son.

You talk about a boy's need to both save and destroy the world. I understand both of these and can see this in my husband. But our little guy is much more docile than most boys. What does this mean for him?

Well, remember that these qualities are indicative of boys, not *required* of boys. All boys are different to varying degrees.

For example, I don't have a compelling need to destroy the world; I'm more of a thinker and creator. But I do love to hit baseballs, and when I do, I try to knock the covers off. I want to just smack them with everything I have. I have the same kind of aggression when I ride my mountain bike down winding trails. At the same time, watching football or boxing doesn't interest me. Your boy could be the same way. Nearly all boys have a natural aggression, but it just shows itself in different ways.

Watch your son play something innocuous like tetherball or Whac-A-Mole. Does he get the eye of the tiger? If not, you can help develop this nature in a healthy way by playfully encouraging him to do so. At the Whac-A-Mole game, have dad jokingly say, "Hey, those moles are laughing at you. They want you to hit them. It makes them feel good! Get fierce! Get that one! Now him! Go! Smash those moles, buddy. You got 'em. Way to go, tiger!" This helps your son connect with dad in a special boy way and assures him that he has what it takes to compete in his world.

I try to teach my son a sense of discipline, but my wife will often say that I'm being too hard. How can I do what I think should be done but also honor my wife's perspective?

This is an important question on a common area of dispute between mothers and fathers.

Mom and dad working on discipline together provide a good and healthy balance, but they generally will teach discipline in different ways. Dad is more likely to be more black and white, right and wrong. Mom is more likely to be considerate of circumstances leading to a particular incident: he's tired, she had a bad day at school, he's just acting out because I told him no. Both ways balance and make allowances for each other.

Mom needs to realize that our children need to experience dad's gentle but firm directives because it prepares them for the rigors of life out in the real world. But kids also need to know that dad will cut them some slack here and there. Dad needs to let mom comfort the children and sometimes make allowances for circumstances; in doing so she's teaching the kids about the uniquely feminine focus on caring and relationships.

The best approach comes down to understanding the important and essential parenting differences between moms and dads and providing children with good, balanced doses of both firm boundaries and situational grace.

———

You talked about boys needing to be innovative, to make things themselves with no help from anyone. I've definitely noticed this in my son. He's not interested in my helping him the first time he does something, like sawing a piece of wood. He just wants to show me that he's capable of doing it by himself. My question is, why doesn't he want me to show him? It's one of the cool things about being a dad.

You've recognized something important about boys. In their drive for independence, they don't want you to show them how to accomplish a task. They want to do it on their own, even when they have never done it before.

Both moms and dads need to recognize this quality and make allowances for it. That means letting your son make appropriate mistakes.

For example, my son sees me trimming the bushes, and he wants to do it. When I try to tell him how, he has no time for it. He wants to get to work proving himself. Depending on the task, I often let him go ahead and try. It's fine if he does something wrong and gets frustrated. That's when I ask if he wants to learn a cool trick. Notice that I don't ask if he wants to "learn how to do it the right way." Then I show him how to hold and use the tool and encourage him to try again.

If you're cutting wood with a chainsaw, I don't recommend the "let him go for it" technique. With dangerous activities, he needs to know that proper training and practice are essential; if he's not willing to submit to the training, he's out of luck. But with other things, let him give it a shot. He will quickly learn by himself that many tasks are harder than they look. Encourage him by saying you will teach him to do it like a pro. Few boys will refuse that kind of challenge.

Much of growing up, for boys and girls, is self-discovery. This approach helps your boy discover himself in a way that is safe but also leaves a lasting impression.

FOUR

What a Girl Needs Most

I have this curious ring in my nose, and I'm happy to have it. It attaches me to a wonderful woman as well as to our children, and it makes me a better and happier man.

I think I first sensed the ring when Jackie and I met during our teen years. She had this mysterious feminine power that attracted and enchanted me. Over time, the same power influenced and formed me in numerous positive ways. I find it interesting that people in the feminist movement think this power that women naturally have over men is some kind of weakness! The one who says yes or no to the interests and desires of a man is indeed powerful. This is true in areas far beyond the romantic and sexual sides of life.

That's exactly what Jackie did to me. Mirroring the male response from day one in every place in the universe where men and women are found, when Jackie exercised this power over me, all I wanted to do was seek to please her in order to spend time with and be close to her. It's no mere sentimental statement to say that I am who I am today because of who God brought to me. This young, amazing red-headed woman befriended me and helped me gain the confidence I needed to stretch myself and try new things—like going to college, becoming an academic, and trying my hand at being an author—simply because of what she saw in me and invested in me over all these years.

Funny thing about that ring in my nose. I've never felt that it is enslavement. In fact, it's a liberator. Research shows this is true for nearly all men. Sociologists have a fancy name for this "female influence over males for the better," calling it "social control."[1] The stronger social control across cultures is nearly always exercised by woman over man rather than man over woman. Ask any older married man, and he will chuckle and tell you it's called "knowing who's the boss!" Genuinely strong, mature, and confident men wouldn't have it any other way.

In addition to being married to a powerful woman, I have the honor of raising four emerging women with her, and that's a great job.

About a Girl

As we consider the miracle of girls, we must recognize the fundamental essence of what we are celebrating. What is a girl? What is a woman? What is important for our children to know about girls on the road to womanhood?

The first thing to know for sure about a girl is this: *a girl is fundamentally a young female on her way to womanhood.* Can you find anything narrow minded, life limiting, or needlessly traditional about this understanding of girlhood? In fact, this simple definition is a very empowering statement for girls because women are powerful beings. Those who would object to such a statement actually have a very low view of women and certainly don't deserve your ear or your daughter's.

GIRLS IN GOD'S IMAGE

The second thing to know for sure about a girl is that she is profoundly powerful because of her creation. The very thing that makes our little guys so important and special also makes our girls so powerful, but in a very intentionally different way. In the first chapter of Genesis, God states, "Let Us make man in Our image, according to Our likeness" (verse 26).

God declares that He will create something possessing a grand distinction from all the rest of His breathtaking creation—a physical and finite being to show forth His invisible and infinite likeness and image in the world. All of creation must have held still in hushed anticipation to see what would represent the King of all creation, the God of all reality. God doesn't hesitate to tell us what this creature is: "So God created man in His own image; in the image of God He created him; male and female He created them" (verse 27).

Male and female He created them! This is one of the grandest statements in all of language.

This creature we know as female, woman, is an image bearer of God's very nature and image in the world. She bears God's image in a way that man simply cannot and never will. God made her this way, with a special standing and power.

As you did with your boy, right now or as soon as you can, call your girl to stand before you for a few moments. *Behold her!* This amazing girl of yours is God's message to you and the whole world of what His image and likeness is, and she communicates that message in a way that no man ever can. In fact, in your daughter's unique design, she also does it in a way that no other woman can either. God has given your girl a combination of gifts, talents, passions, and personality that no one else in time has or will have. She is mold-breaking amazing. Now tell her this so she can grasp this reality and truth about herself. Tell her to let her female humanness be the foundation and fountain of her self-perception. As we mentioned in the previous chapter, the verse we just read is a divine declaration that the male-female distinction in humanity is fundamental to our God-imaging purpose. We don't know *how* exactly, but we know it is because God said so.

So what are the things that make girls on the road to womanhood distinct and fascinating creatures? What are the genuine female qualities of a good, healthy girl on her way to womanhood? And as the parents of your remarkable girl, how can you nudge her along the way?

Girls Need to See Themselves as Capable, Not Victims

Much of the feminist movement has tried to define women as victims of male domination. If they think that's a smart and healthy position to assume, they can have it. The truth is that healthy women are not comfortable being victims and won't settle for it. Like anyone, healthy women certainly face troubles and mistreatment, but they don't let that define them. They have confidence in their own dignity and power to struggle to remove themselves from troubling circumstances and to rise above their trials. I think of three very different women who faced great challenges in life.

As a young woman, Anne Frank faced incredible trauma, degradation, and finally murder with a strength and honor I'm not sure I could have summoned as a middle-aged man.

Rosa Parks faced dehumanizing humiliation all her life, until one day she decided to simply not take it anymore. She became a sign of strength and moral courage, and her actions served as a spark to ignite a dramatically important American movement.

Jacqueline Bouvier Kennedy, a woman of immense privilege and power, had every right to assume the position of victim following the horribly violent death of her husband before the world. But she rose above it all and carried herself to her last day with matchless dignity and grace.

What to Teach Your Girl About Being Capable

Our girls should learn from us by both word and example that they are too strong, valuable, and capable to ever become victims. Our girls should become what they are called and created to become, rather than what some special-interest group or advertiser says they should be. The constant, unconditional love and affirmation of both mom and dad produce this kind of confidence, repelling the shackles of victimhood.

As parents, we need to help our daughters navigate the hurts, doubts, and struggles of these kinds of challenges so that they learn two primary truths:

1. You can overcome nearly anything that comes your way if you resolve to do so and believe you have the support of caring and thoughtful people behind you.
2. You are stronger and made of bigger stuff than the arrows and roadblocks that come your way.

GIRLS WANT TO BE THE MOST IMPORTANT PERSON IN THE WORLD TO A MAN

A team member of mine at work told me that as a single woman—and a very confident and capable professional woman with a gigantic sense of humor—the hardest part of losing her dad was that she was no longer the most important person in the world to a particular man. That struck me profoundly. From her earliest years, she had always felt that her dad delighted in her and believed she set the sun. Now he is gone, and there is no man to replace him in this esteem for her. She flies home regularly to visit her mom and returns with great stories of their time together. But her mom is not her dad.

Like my co-worker, girls and women can be content in themselves. But they are wired to find contentment in being important to men also. In fact, each woman needs to be uniquely important to one particular, special man. Usually this man is first her father. When the woman gets married, she then has two men who are crazy about her. (And she can trust that if her husband doesn't treat her right, he will have her dad to reckon with.)

What to Teach Your Girl About Being the Most Important Person in the World to a Man

Is your girl the most important person in the world to the key man in her life? Who is that man, and is he a good man? Does she really know what she means to this man? He should tell her.

I tell my girls that I hope they will one day meet and marry amazing, funny, kind, sacrificing men. But the number one requirement will be that he doesn't mind my being the most important man in their lives. What's more, they will have to be okay with my being around all the time. I say I will probably go on vacation with them, drop by for dinner a few times a week, and take them to lunch as well. I'll hang out at their places of work just to be close to them. I warn them I have every intention of being there on the scene as these girls become women, and their husbands will just have to deal with it.

Of course, my daughters know I'm teasing, and they tease right back.

Even so, they hear me saying that my heart is smitten with them. Even after they have given themselves completely to another man in marriage, I will still be there pursuing them as well. My girls gain great confidence in this, and it will certainly affect how they choose and dismiss candidates for husbands. They know I set the bar high because they are great treasures. In turn, they set the bar high for themselves.

GIRLS NEED INTIMACY

We all need love: boys and girls, men and women. Love is the first requirement of humanity because we are created in the image of Love: a divine community of Father, Son, and Holy Spirit, who love eternally and intensely.

But when it comes to human intimacy, girls have a greater need to be intimate than boys do. Girls want to both offer and receive intimacy (as opposed to boys, who more want to *have* intimacy) because *being* intimate is a part of their essence. I'm not talking about intimacy as sexual; that's only one kind of intimacy. I'm talking about an emotional, personal connection, about being received, heard, and understood by others.

Carl Jung once observed, "Loneliness does not come from having no people about one, but from being unable to communicate the things that seem important to oneself."[2] In other words, loneliness is the absence of people who are interested in and want to understand you. In a sense, girls are more likely to value being involved in such relationships, while boys are more likely to want to get something done, even if with a friend.

Take sports. For a young boy, being on his first team is about his identity. His team ball cap proudly announces that to the world. It's also about maturity: "I'm a real baseball player now, and we wear real uniforms!" And it's about learning skills—fielding, throwing, hitting.

For a girl, sports teams and the like are about connection: "I love my teammates! I love the team I'm on." It's also about friendships. This isn't to say that boys don't make friends on teams or that girls aren't interested in learning new skills. But whether on a sports team or at school or at work when they grow into women, girls will be more content in life with a handful of truly meaningful relationships; this intimacy is more defining for them.

What to Teach Your Girl About Intimacy

Our girls must learn that intimacy—physical or emotional—is never something they earn from or owe to anyone. Intimacy is a gift they give to and receive from others. They will decide who is safe and trustworthy with such intimacies, both physical and emotional.

Our girls learn not to be controlled by others in the giving and receiving of friendship, intimacy, and love when they learn from both mom and dad that intimacy and closeness are never devices to manipulate or control. In fact, love and friendship can only be defined as real intimacy when they are freely given. Our daughters should expect this from themselves and others.

GIRLS NEED COMMUNITY

Connected to the need for intimacy is a girl's great need for the group. Your girl needs to have her posse, her own little community. This especially happens around the fourth to sixth grade. Of course, if one girl in the group feels slighted, talked about, or left out, there's going to be trouble. I wonder if teachers of these grade levels should get additional combat or mediator pay for the time, energy, and cunning they invest to sort out the nearly daily girlfriend squabbles.

These squabbles happen because girls this age are navigating the important waters of maturity between what each wants and needs as an individual girl and what the group wants and needs as girls. This important learning time provides girls with many of the essential character qualities they'll need in their later and deeply rewarding woman communities. Being a part of these groups provides a necessary life education and experience for girls.

What to Teach Your Girl About Community

Our daughters need to learn that the female communities they develop in early adulthood will be rich pools of happiness and connectedness for decades to come. The groups of their late elementary and middle school years teach them valuable lessons for the communities they join later in life. They can learn to choose wisely in knowing which groups to invest in and commit themselves to. Can the girls in the group help your girl become who she wants to be? Can your daughter give herself to the other girls in dedication and friendship and trust them to care for and help develop her feminine soul, heart, and mind? Will the girls build good and healthy things into her merely by her relationships with them? She needs a group of girls who can do all of these things, and she needs to offer the same to others.

GIRLS NEED TO MOTHER

Many young women who grew up during the feminist movement are making different life choices today. What are they focusing on? They are certainly interested in careers, yet they are also doing what they can to make sure their careers don't eclipse their lives as mothers.[3]

These women live for a different set of priorities as a way of personal fulfillment; this fulfillment increasingly involves the birth, rearing, and care of children. Some women are even doing so without getting a husband first, as their biological clocks are ticking faster than their wedding bells are ringing. As one high-powered, impressively employed single mom from Manhattan told me, "I am really quite conservative and traditional in my family views. I have a wonderful and successful career, but what I want most is to be a mom." She continued, "I want a husband too, and my child to have a dad, definitely. But he hasn't shown up yet, so I need to have my baby before my time runs out." This growing sentiment is seen in the skyrocketing rates of cohabitation and unmarried childbearing among twenty- and thirty-something women.[4]

The female brain is hard-wired for motherhood. The need to be a mom is found in the influence of oxytocin, an important chemical that surges in your daughter's brain at very early ages. You know that oxytocin is present when she responds to something that needs care and comfort: a baby doll, a puppy, a pet rabbit, a stuffed animal, and as she grows, a baby crying within earshot. Oxytocin is the bonding hormone. It also kicks in later when your daughter becomes interested in boys. Again, it helps her bond at this stage. Her oxytocin will elevate when she hears a baby cry, more upon seeing the baby, and it really gets coursing when she is able to hold and cuddle the baby. Oxytocin is what's at work in a nursing mother when she hears a baby cry other than her own and can feel her milk start to move. The result of this chemical's effect is the mothering instinct that flows through women's hearts, brains, and every part of their makeup.

What to Teach Your Girl About Mothering

The first thing our girls should learn about mothering is that the word *just* should never be used anywhere near the word *mother*. There's no such thing as "just a mother." How did we ever come to the place where conceiving, growing, nourishing, birthing, nursing, and raising a new, unique, and complex human being could ever be qualified by the word *just*? Only moms possess the power to mother. So this quality should be a greater point of womanly pride.

We certainly don't need to force younger girls into mothering as we might do with kids and sports. They already have a heart that moves to mother, care for, and protect. Along with their other life interests and passions, this quality will develop as they grow.

As parents, we need to let our girls be the kind of mommas they want to be, at their own pace. Even girls who seem to have little interest in dolls and mothering are by no means unhealthy. It might simply be that this part of their femaleness is not as strong as for other girls.

GIRLS WANT TO BE THE PRETTIEST ONE IN THE ROOM

While a man might desire to be "the smartest guy in the room" or "the one with the best stories," women are more likely to first size themselves up by seeing who among all the women is most attractive!

Confident and healthy women realize they have a great power and allure in their physical attractiveness, because it can attract, impact, and lure men without their ever lifting a finger or speaking a word.

For most girls, being pretty is basic stuff. We certainly haven't pushed this with our daughters in any way. When they were young, we dressed them in little jeans and Old Navy or GapKids tees and clogs. But when our girls got to about ten or eleven, something came alive in them. The time it takes for them to get ready to go anywhere increased exponentially. *Everything* has to be just right; if not, then they aren't going anywhere until it is! Schaeffer literally tumbles out of bed five minutes before we leave for school. He fusses over himself by *maybe* brushing his teeth and running his fingers through his hair!

No doubt, you've seen this quality with your daughters, and you are astonished that the interest in "being pretty" develops without the slightest prodding from anyone. If anything, your only influence is to put the brakes on a bit to keep it all in perspective.

What to Teach Your Girl About Being the Prettiest One in the Room

We must teach our girls that their inherent value is not their beauty. It's fine to want to look nice, for this is their nature. But their appearance shouldn't define them.

Our girls also must learn the power of their femininity, which is like the seasoning in a fine meal or the instrumentation in a ballet or symphony. Bold and stark is fun, but only occasionally. Understated is where the real magic and beauty is found. Show your daughter examples of this, compared to over-the-top girls.

Our girls (and boys) absorb a great deal from us fathers about the kinds of women we find smart and attractive; it starts with how we talk about and respond to their moms, our wives.

GIRLS NEED MODESTY

There's a funny scene in the movie *Jerry Maguire,* where Jerry goes to the locker room to talk to football star Rod Tidwell about working together. As they talk, Rod comes out of the shower and just stands there in front of Jerry, buck naked and dripping wet. Jerry uncomfortably says, "Towel?" Rod picks up instantly on Jerry's uneasy cue and coolly assures him all is good by saying, "No, I air dry."

Not many guys choose to air dry, but *no* girls ever would. Girls are simply modest. Women, young and old, have a sense that their physical nature and uniqueness is not something to be ashamed of. Yet they also sense that there's something special, perhaps even sacred, in their physical form. They recognize it as a jewel to be protected and guarded. Even women in primitive tribes that we see in *National Geographic* or on the Discovery Channel most definitely have a sense of modesty as well, even though it might be quite different than ours. In her deeply researched and smartly written book *A Return to Modesty,* Wendy Shalit explains that modesty in various cultures with differing clothing traditions is about context and intention.[5] Shalit notes that where both men and women adorn themselves with only leaves or a garment of animal skin around their waists, a very important and rigid code of modesty still exists. In many tribes, the women wouldn't think of changing an old leaf apron for new without first removing themselves to complete seclusion from other men and women. In addition, men and women in these cultures have proper and improper ways of looking upon one another. Doing so improperly is a dramatic personal and cultural transgression.

We have similar codes of modesty in our culture that seem normal to us. For example, a halter top and shorts for a woman might actually be a modest choice for a trip to the beach, compared to a bikini. But wearing the same clothing to pop into the office to get something on your day off or to a parent-teacher meeting would be improper.

Girls aren't modest because it's preferable. Modesty is a deeper part of feminine essence, and healthy women take the power and gift of their femininity seriously in order to protect it.

What to Teach Your Girl About Modesty

As parents, we need to teach our girls that modesty is a positive, confident, and noble virtue. Modesty isn't prudish, insecure, or reactive. Help your daughter understand that her feeling for and sense of modesty is a measure of the esteem that she has for herself, for the gift of womanhood that God gave her, and for how she expects others to view her.

Help your daughter understand what modesty is, how it honors the essence of a woman, and how it is well modeled by mothers, sisters, and other women. Help her understand that modesty isn't a style, like some of the "uniforms" some Christian women adopt as a false badge of spirituality. Nothing is particularly sacred about denim jumpers or a certain length or cut of hair. Instead, modesty is about protecting and adorning a woman's beauty. It keeps the beauty of a woman honorable rather than turning it into something tawdry.

Every parent should read Wendy Shalit's *A Return to Modesty*. In fact, making this book required reading as a rite of passage for our young people would do a world of good in deepening our humanity.

GIRLS ARE CAREGIVERS AND LESS IMPULSIVE

The hormone serotonin saves us more on car insurance than Geico ever could. The increased level of serotonin in the female brain is what moves your daughter toward being less impulsive than your son. She will be more measured, more reticent, more cautious, and better able to focus longer on one task because the serotonin coursing through her brain is a powerful impulse inhibitor. She is also less likely to be a chance taker.

Serotonin also works with the higher levels of oxytocin in a girl's brain to drive her toward caregiving. In her toddler years, she'll want to take care of baby dolls or stuffed animals. If she can't find one of these, she'll invent something to cuddle, comfort, dress, feed, change, take to the doctor, teach, and generally care for. She doesn't do this simply because she sees mom do it and imitates her. Even mothers who deliberately share caregiving tasks evenly with their husbands, thinking all such things are taught to daughters, find their girls naturally becoming little miss mommas.

In her book *The Female Brain,* Louann Brizendine writes of seeing this in her practice. She tells of one mother who was concerned, even though she gave her three-year-old daughter only unisex toys to play with, she walked into her daughter's room one day and found her cradling a bright red fire truck in her arms. The little girl was calming it with the assuring words, "Don't worry, little truckie, everything will be all right." Brizendine explains,

> This isn't socialization. This little girl didn't cuddle her "truckie" because her environment molded her unisex brain.… She was born with a female brain, which came complete with its own impulses. Girls arrive already wired as girls, and boys arrive already wired as boys.[6]

Girls and women need and want to make a personal difference to others. They want to impact *people,* while boys and men want to impact *situations.* Both affect people but in different ways. Consider an emergency situation like a house fire. Men will be driven to rescue the people and stop the fire. Rescuing the people from a burning house, the man will carry them to a safe location, put them down, and turn to go back into the house without even seeming to check on their status. He knows others in the house need to be rescued. A woman, however, will instinctively check on the status on the individual victims and make sure they are properly cared for.

What to Teach Your Girl About Caregiving and Being Impulsive

Like many things about our girls, we need to help them understand that these womanly qualities such as caregiving and caution are not weaknesses but incredible strengths. Too often we unintentionally accept our culture's message that these characteristics are more womanly and therefore weaker, but we should help our girls understand why these are remarkable human strengths that will enhance their lives tremendously as they grow older. Therefore, our girls should have fun with these qualities now.

The desire and impulse toward caregiving is one of the highest human qualities; humans spend more of their lives caring for their young than any other creature on earth. Caregiving is deeply human and profoundly consequential, and women are gifted with a greater ability to undertake it than men are.

Our boys should also be taught to see caregiving as a strength. For boys, we should focus on teaching this more in their teens, after their boy natures have been well developed and they can learn that caregiving can be very masculine in its service to others. A simple but great example is Jesus, who washed the feet of His followers, very much a servant's task but also powerfully masculine.

GIRLS ARE EMOTIONALLY PERCEPTIVE

The female brain is created to be more aware of and better able to read the emotions, facial expressions, and body language of others. Michael Gurian notes, "Even in infancy, from as young as four months old, girls can better distinguish family members' faces from photographs they look at. Boys have more trouble."[7] He also explains that even at one week old, girls are better able to note and respond to another baby's cry than boys are. Brizendine explains that baby girls more strongly connect with the faces of those around them, while boys connect with the objects and action around them. Their distinctive male and female brains drive them in these two different ways of connecting.[8]

This explains something that has perplexed nearly all wives and mothers. How many wives have asked their husbands incredulously, "Don't you hear that baby crying?" "Baby crying" can be replaced with "dog barking" or "phone ringing." Men can seem oblivious, but in their defense, this is exactly how God made them.

What to Teach Your Girl About Being Emotionally Perceptive

Our girls should accept their heightened ability to read others' emotions and facial expressions as a hidden superpower that makes them more capable of being able to relate to others, better aware of what's going on around them. This perceptiveness is a strong part of a woman's intuition and one of the reasons girls are more likely to be settled and attentive in their elementary classes than boys. They are more comfortably and confidently cued to the flow of the classroom and the state and expectations of their teacher.

Boys need to learn about this stronger perceptive sense girls possess because they will need this knowledge as men. I must confess there have been many times when I thought Jackie overreacted to things—and she will tell you that sometimes she does. But most times she is doing what women naturally do: perceiving the cues of voice tone, body movement, facial expression, eye movement, tilt of the head, folded arms or hands on hips, the way things are phrased. Women take all these in and can read how someone is doing and feeling. This can be a volatile area for dating and married men and women, and it can be very helpful for both to know what's at work.

GIRLS NEED TO TALK

Related to a girl's stronger perception and emotional antennae is the need to talk. Note that I said "talk" rather than "communicate." Both men and women have the need to communicate, but they do it differently.

Women talk. They are greater word users, because the language center in a woman's brain is larger than a man's by about a third. Scientists are also finding a larger and stronger wiring connection in female brains between the areas where emotions are processed and those that process language; in fact, this connection is about 25 percent greater in females than in males. Louann Brizendine's two excellent books *The Female Brain* and *The Male Brain* explain how male and female brains are very different even before birth. The books sport very interestingly illustrated cover art: both feature images that unmistakably resemble the human brain, complete with brainstem. The brain on the male book is fashioned with duct tape as its artistic medium, signifying that men are more results oriented and need to fix things. The brain on the female brain book is a telephone cord formed in the shape of the brain, signifying that women say, "I am, therefore I talk."

Girls need to talk because talking is one of their primary ways of connecting. Jackie has a good friend, Sandy, who has kids the same ages as ours. Both are stay-at-home moms. Every few months, Jackie and Sandy get to steal a "girls' night out."

About 10:00 p.m., Sandy's van will pull into the driveway, and they will just sit and talk for a while. One night when this happened, I went to bed, knowing Jackie was safely home and would be in shortly. I was startled out of sleep at about 2:30 a.m. by some noise in our room, and I realized that Jackie wasn't next to me. The noise turned out to be her changing into her pajamas. I asked her if she'd been downstairs watching television all this time, thinking maybe she couldn't sleep.

She said, "No, Sandy and I just got done talking."

I thought, *Good for you. I'm glad you had that time.*

If I'd told Jackie I'd had a conversation of that length with one of my friends, she'd know that some serious issue needed discussing, and she would naturally ask me what was wrong. And she would be correct in her perception. But with Jackie and Sandy, I knew such a question would be far too dramatic for this scenario. They simply took advantage of the opportunity for uninterrupted talk.

What to Teach Your Girl About Needing to Talk

Both boys and girls need to learn that girls make more use of words not because they're unable to construct or organize thoughts economically but simply because they talk the way they are wired to talk. Our girls need that confidence in themselves and how they are created. Girls also need to be aware of the difference in the ways boys and girls communicate so they can be aware that their style of talk might not easily be understood by their opposite-sex peers.

Where I work, we have had many women in key leadership positions. A few of them by nature are as direct and to the point as most men are. But others are much more "stereotypical" female. They tell great and detailed stories that fill the room with energy, emotion, and honesty. I like that these women are comfortable and confident being themselves and don't feel that they have be "more like men in a man's world." Some co-workers, both men and women, wonder why these women leaders go on in such a way. But most of us glory in it, seeing them as confident and comfortable women. And that's a very healthy perspective to teach our children.

GIRLS NEED TO BE HEARD AND AFFIRMED

Being heard is one characteristic that is equally important to both girls and boys, but in very different ways. God has given each of us the gift of communication. We must understand that communication is a deeply special, divine, and sacred thing. I am serious and not overstating this one degree. Let me explain.

Think about the fundamental and eternal natures and qualities of God. Because we are speaking of God, these are countless. But that doesn't mean we can't understand many of them. For our discussion here, we know God is not solitary, but Three in One; even before creation, God existed in eternal relationship. Jesus told us as much when He said that His Father has loved Him, the Son, from "before the foundation of the world" (John 17:24). Part of this divine relationship involved personal communion and communication, because we know God isn't static and impersonal; He's an intensely personal, relational God who speaks. On the first page of our Bibles, our first introduction to God and creation finds God speaking His intention to create and then speaking His creation into being. Communication isn't a created thing or merely human. It's deeply divine and eternal, something given to each of us as part of our image-bearing humanity.

This is all foundational when we consider how and why it's particularly important for girls to be heard and affirmed. As we just discussed, talking is more basic to a girl's being. The other side of talking is being heard and affirmed in thoughts and communicated feelings. So talking and being heard is a significant way for women to gain their sense of significance, worth, belonging, and connection. At the same time, it's more painful and damaging for girls if they sense they are not being heard or that what they have to say isn't worth considering.

What to Teach Your Girl About Being Heard and Affirmed

We need to communicate to our girls how smart and articulate they are. Mom's listening and interested responses are important because through them our girls are being adopted into and learning about being part of a community of women. Dad's listening and interested responses build into our girls a rich and necessary sense of confidence in talking to men—even debating sometimes—so they learn to hold their own, as well as what it means to be accepted and taken seriously by a man. This is a key life lesson for a girl.

Our girls also must learn that they have a right to speak up as much as anyone in any setting. Sure, they must be mindful of not interrupting or inserting themselves into a conversation that's for adults, and they need to understand the etiquette of when talking is and is not appropriate. But they must learn that they have good thoughts worth sharing at appropriate times. One of the ways parents can help with this is to ask their girls about their thoughts on the topic being discussed in a group. A parent might ask her daughter to share something she said earlier: "Tess, tell Mr. and Mrs. Simpson what you told me yesterday about the way that school in California is handling…" Your daughter will gain great confidence by your recognition that she has something worth saying, and even greater confidence by seeing that she can speak to others who find the conversation interesting and worth listening to.

GIRLS NEED A SENSE OF SECURITY

This girl quality actually surprised me. When doing interviews for this book, I talked with a lot of women from various walks and stations of life as well as various cultures. One of the questions I asked is, "Do women have the need to be taken care of?"

To be honest, I expected to be strictly corrected by women on this, particularly independent women who have no obvious need to be taken care of by anyone. But that's not what I found.

A flight attendant on a flight back from New York City asked me what I was writing, and we started to talk about the subject of this book.

I asked her if she thought it was true that women had a need to be taken care of. She responded as if that weren't even a question. She told me warmly how her father was her source of security and care. She said her brothers were often too protective and controlling and she was glad she received confidence and a sense of strong independence from her father. As a single woman, she was thankful for these men in her life and the sense of safety they provided. She added that she desired to have such a man in her life now.

The need for women to feel safe and cared for is reflected in the orientation of the female body. It receives, protects, and covers, and therefore she is protective. She wants to make sure bad folks stay out. It's doubtful any human felt more secure, safe, protected, and defended anyplace than in our mothers' wombs. Therefore, it's no coincidence that women need a sense of security and safety more than men do. Their bodies, as well as their brains, are created this way.

What to Teach Your Girl About a Sense of Security

Our girls should never see their need for security and safety as a weakness; certainly, they should never apologize for it or put on an artificial brave front. To do so is to deny their feminine nature.

Our girls do well to realize that true manliness and its twin brother, gentlemanliness, exist only because women exist. These male qualities exist for the singular reason that women are worth treasuring and protecting. That again is a power women possess that they should celebrate.

THE DESTINY OF YOUR GIRL

Womanhood is powerful in no small part because it is the destiny of your little girl. Our girls must learn comfort and confidence in the power of their femininity. Both mom and dad play irreplaceable roles here but in importantly different ways.

Well-adjusted girls typically come from well-adjusted mothers, or sometimes from an aunt or grandmother who is secure and comfortable in her womanness. From these women, our girls learn the ins and outs of womanhood. Moms help girls develop their own unique sense of womanhood, both by setting healthy examples and also by serving as examples of how not to be. This can take a dramatic form: "I will never be an alcoholic (or victim of domestic violence) like my mother." But it also has milder forms: "I don't want to be as negative (or as gossipy) as my mother." Most mothers, as well as fathers, typically serve their children in both those positive- and negative-example ways, and this is natural and helpful, given that no parent is perfect. Moms are influential, and most often when they are unaware of it. Our daughters need that influence.

From their fathers, our girls develop a different and yet extremely important kind of confidence—one based on a definite sense of personal value, worth, and significance. Mom is more likely to give her girls confidence *as* a woman. Dad gives his daughters confidence because they *are* women. That's a powerful confidence. A confident girl knows who she is and rests in the reality that she has the love, affection, and esteem of a good and honorable man—her father.

Girls who don't have this dad security are more likely to end up being a slave to endless, embarrassing, and failing efforts at attracting and impressing boys in early life and men in later life. They get used horribly, and this sends them into deeper self-doubt and loathing.

Show me a girl who is secure, confident, kind, and inclusive to others, and I will show you a girl with a connected and affirming dad in her life.

YOUR AMAZING GIRL

Your son and daughter both need to understand that girls are amazing. Our boys need to learn the qualities that make girls amazing so they can gain and demonstrate the proper respect for women (and one day, their own wives and daughters). Girls need to learn these amazing qualities so they understand the fullness of their incredible nature and gain confidence in it.

These inherent female qualities are largely universal for women in all cultures. They might manifest themselves in different ways, but the quality and essence is there. The list is not exhaustive, for the mystery of being feminine can hardly be contained in a list. But here are the most prominent and universal.

- Girls need to see themselves as capable, not victims.
- Girls want to be the most important person in the world to a man.
- Girls need intimacy.
- Girls need community.
- Girls need to mother.
- Girls want to be the prettiest one in the room.
- Girls need modesty.
- Girls are caregivers and less impulsive.
- Girls are more perceptive, reading emotions better.
- Girls need to talk.
- Girls need to be heard and affirmed.
- Girls need a sense of security.

Talk about these qualities with your children. Talk about how you've recognized them in the women you know and how they might recognize them. What are examples of both *healthy* and *unhealthy* demonstrations of these qualities? Which of these are the strengths of the women in your family, and how are they demonstrated? Which are not as strong or prominent in your family? Does this create a deficit in your family? Why or why not?

———

You talked about how both male and female are made in the image of God. How can woman be made in the image and reveal the likeness of a male God? Isn't this just nice imagery that doesn't really mean anything? Or are you trying to feminize God?

This question is important because of the creation narrative that describes where our sex-distinctive humanity comes from.

Let me explain how God can create females in His image. First, even though God communicates Himself as Father and He has many masculine qualities, He is not a *human* person. As such, He doesn't have a male sex distinction as human males do. All of humanity flows from the Trinity of God, and we resemble and image God in many ways. However, we are not an exact image. For example, we were created with appetites for food, and we get hungry. God created us to enjoy collecting, preparing, and eating food. But God doesn't get hungry. He doesn't have an appetite as we do. This difference doesn't make us any less "made in His image." The same is true for men and women; even though male and female are different from each other, both are created in God's image.

———

You talked about a girl's need to be the most important person in the world to a man. I can totally relate to that, as that is what I was in my father's eyes. It meant the world to me. I now have two daughters going into their teen years, and their father isn't around. We divorced four years ago, and he hasn't been involved in their lives. How can I make up for this significant gap in my daughters' lives and help them experience what I experienced with my father?

While only a dad can be a dad, some men can come closer than others to filling this role for your daughters. Regardless of who might play this role in their lives, the fact still remains that their dad isn't on the scene. I say this not to make you feel bad or hopeless but to acknowledge that this dad-sized hole in your children's hearts can only be imperfectly filled by someone else. However, imperfectly filled doesn't mean it's not worth trying. We all do things imperfectly, but we keep on, knowing that good is much better than not at all.

The first man to look to is your own father, their grandfather. He obviously loved you well. He can be an important and stable man in your girls' lives, giving them that special feeling of significance. If your father is no longer living, I would look to their uncles or other men in your family who might be able to communicate authentic love and appreciation for the remarkable women your girls are. In addition, men who have died can still be present in very real ways. If your father has died, talk to your girls about how he affirmed and loved you and how he would so love the various qualities, talents, and personalities they possess. In fact, don't just tell them; show them by explaining why he would marvel at distinct parts of their womanhood. This builds something important into your daughters!

As you say, girls are relational. But I've seen two of my daughters soak up relationships like a sponge with no real sense of discernment or intentionality. Is this normal for young girls? Should I be concerned?

It is normal for many girls, but it can be unhealthy. Friendships are valuable, but we don't want our girls to seek out and attach to others faster than relationships can reasonably and properly develop. Our children must learn to be discerning and responsible. They should protect themselves from giving their hearts and joy away to someone whom they know very little about. Urge them to ask themselves some basic questions: *Will this be a safe relationship? Is this girl likely to help me become the woman I'm intended to be? Will she bring out unhealthy attitudes and behaviors in me? What will her influence be like?*

These are questions both boys and girls need to ask about new friendships. But given the deeper emotional and relational intensity within tween-girl relationships, our girls especially need to learn this kind of relationship discernment. Many girls pick this up naturally, but if your daughters don't get it themselves and are pursuing relationships you don't feel good about, they absolutely need you to be the parent and protect them from it.

—

I recognize the importance of modesty in our world today, and I want to teach its importance to my daughter. But sometimes I feel uncomfortable doing so. I know that as a dad, I can really help my daughter or I can easily embarrass her and make her uncomfortable. What's the right role for a dad here?

First, it's awesome that a dad is asking this question. The fact that you're sensitive about the benefits of teaching your daughter modesty will help you avoid many of the pitfalls.

One of the biggest roles you can play is affirming your daughter's beauty in natural and fitting ways so that she gains a sense of her own femininity. Do this when she is dressed up for a special occasion but also when she is playing in the backyard on a Saturday afternoon. Let her know she can be beautiful without even really trying. Give her specific examples so she can see that you really notice. And dad, you as a caring, loving man in her life, can help your daughter understand what clothing choices are wise and appropriate for her from a man's perspective. In age-appropriate ways, she needs to understand how to dress, realizing that as a young, emerging woman, she will have an impact on young men, and how to do it so her femininity and personhood is respected and honored.

As girls get this kind of confirmation from this most important man in their lives, the need to dramatically accentuate their looks becomes less intense.

In very appropriate and loving ways, as your daughter grows into womanhood, you can express your pride in how beautiful she is becoming. You can remind her that her beauty can be very powerful to a young man. Talk about when you were a young man and what caused you to respect certain girls and what other girls did to lose your respect.

FIVE

The Journey to Manhood: Making Healthy Men out of Healthy Boys

Isn't he the cutest little guy you've ever seen?" I said to my teen daughter, pointing to a picture on the refrigerator as she fixed dinner for our family one evening. She responded, "Where *did* that boy go to?"

Where did he go, indeed!

I was pointing to Schaeffer's second-grade school picture, which had been made into a magnet that now holds miscellanea to our refrigerator. He had a little skater-boy haircut, a sprinkling of freckles across his nose, and marshmallow cheeks animated and elevated by a smile as bright as the sun. Now he's becoming such a young man, and I love to see him grow every day. He is nearly as tall as I am, his voice is growing deep, and he is far smarter and more mature than I was at his age.

Where, oh where, did my little boy go?

LIFE'S NONSTOP CONVEYOR BELT

No doubt you've asked the same thing about your child. As parents, we realize that our children are on a conveyer belt called life. Once started, it just doesn't stop. There's no off switch, no pause button. As much as we might want to keep our little ones little, we can't. Once the conveyor belt of life starts, it keeps moving. The irony is that we want it to move on and stay still at the same time.

Adolescence, which means "to grow," is a relatively new life stage in human history. More than one hundred years ago, our children went more directly from childhood to adulthood. But now adolescence is the primary window from which boys emerge into manhood and girls into womanhood. This means we want to consider the male and female paths during this important stretch on the conveyor belt.

My goal in this and the following chapter is to help mothers and fathers develop an appreciation for how important and difficult the transition from adolescence into adulthood can be and how to help our daughters and sons walk through it with as much direction and guidance as possible, and in sex-specific ways. Remember, God has not just given you a little human to raise into mature, healthy, and productive adulthood; He has given you a little male human or a little female human.

What kind of men will our boys become?

What kind of women will our girls become?

Why We Need to Grow Healthy Men

Adolescence is a vitally important transitional life stage. When boys enter adolescence, their hormones start to surge again, similar to when they were growing in the secret of the womb and things started really happening to their bodies. These are the two great hormonal growth spurts of life. During the adolescent years, our boys learn some consequential lessons. Many of these lessons are likely to "set" like concrete during this period, based on how and whether they learn them well or not. This is an important parenting stage as well, but one that too many parents sit out because they aren't sure what to do or because they believe they can't have any real influence. But parents are the ones who can have the greatest and most important influence.

In the amazing project of creating men from boys, we do well to recognize a curious fact about every single boy who has ever come forth into the world, including your own: not one of them has ever been a man before! As a rule, people who have never done something before need some help and direction in learning how to do it. Few pick it up all by themselves.

Who will help your little boy become a man? How will this be achieved? These are profound parenting questions that demand great and long reflection. Note that I wasn't entirely correct earlier. Each conveyor belt leads not necessarily to manhood but to male aging, because that's what the mere passage of time produces. But good men don't just happen. Good men are most often created in good families, and great intention needs to be put into the process. Fathers and other men play a key role!

Our boys are on an inevitable conveyer belt toward some kind of adult life. They can be carried to an adult life of either healthy manhood or a narcissistic and indulgent male adolescence. Which will it be for your boy? Intentional motherhood and fatherhood will make all the difference.

In my work at Focus on the Family, I spend the greater part of my workdays looking at the social problems and influences that are eroding family and society. I've come to believe that the most pressing problem is one that few recognize. Marriage and family are declining so badly in nearly all American communities because, as a society, we have forgotten how to manufacture good men. Good men do what's right, and they respect and care for the women in their lives. They work hard, they don't make excuses, they know what their duties are, and they do them without complaining. They fight for what is right and hold accountable those who do wrong, including themselves.

If women can't find good men to marry, they will instead compromise themselves by merely living with a make-do man or getting babies from him without marriage. Unfortunately, this describes exactly the new shape of family growth in Western nations by exploding margins: unmarried cohabitation and unmarried childbearing by twenty-, thirty-, and even forty-something women far outpace any other family formation trend in terms of growth over the last ten years.[1] Women want to marry and have daddies for their babies. But if they can't find good men to commit themselves to, well… Our most pressing social problem today is a man deficit.

This explains why one of the most important social roles of the family—both for an individual as well as the larger community—is to produce good men from boys.[2] If that's our role, then what should both mothers and fathers—as well as other involved adults like teachers, neighbors, coaches, and scout leaders—be mindful of as our boys move along this conveyer to male adulthood? What are the key things our boys need in order to reach the destination that their future wives, children, and communities need them to reach?

Boys Must Recognize the Destination

Any journey must first begin by knowing where you are headed and why. This is certainly true for a boy's journey into manhood. How many boys think that manhood simply means growing old enough to drive, legally drink, eat what he wants, sleep late, and go to the kinds of movies he wants? While this kind of adulthood is a destination, it's not much of one.

On their journey into manhood, our boys need to have a destination worthy of the gift of masculinity that God has given them, rather than one merely handed to them—like military orders they're expected to dutifully fulfill without question. Your son's destination must be developed in connection with your son and the kind of male God has created him to be. Both mom and dad should make this journey a continual conversation with him, with thousands of both great and small installments through your boy's toddler, elementary, adolescent, teen, and young adult years. These can take the form of simple discussions or comments at any of these ages when you encounter men who do or do not exemplify healthy, balanced manhood.

Consider Willie Morris, the main character in the really wonderful movie *My Dog Skip.* As a young guy, Willie isn't every dad's picture of the ideal boy. He's small and fragile, a bit of a momma's boy, but very sweet, smart, kind, and imaginative. He grows up to really make something of himself. Watch this movie with your son, and talk about Willie's dad, artfully played by Kevin Bacon. Is he a good man? Why or why not? Is he strong? loving? What does your son think is good about the dad? What does your boy like about Willie? What about Willie's boyhood hero? How does Willie become a good man?

Others movies like *A River Runs Through It* and *About a Boy* are good for dads and sons to watch and discuss, especially when boys are in their midteens. The Johnny Depp version of *Charlie and the Chocolate Factory* and *Little Manhattan* are good films to view and talk about with younger boys. What do these movies teach us about becoming a man? How well did the guys in these movies do in their journeys?

You can also find examples of a boy's emergence into manhood in real life, books, shows, music, and sports. Talk with your son about the strengths and weaknesses of these examples. These don't have to be fully good or completely bad stories. Help your son discern the good and desirable from that which he should avoid and to understand the why of both. Mom, tell your son stories about their uncles and grandfathers. Dad, tell your son stories about your own journey into manhood. Your boy will eat it up!

Both parents should be straightforward in explaining what good men absolutely do and what they don't do. Remember that some things along these lines will be matters of personality. Many boys will want to learn how to field dress a deer or elk, but this isn't essential to being a good man. Some boys won't show an interest in reading, but all boys should be readers of some sort. Not all boys will like football or baseball, but boys should learn to be comfortable and somewhat competent at various sports. In fact, the competitive engagement is probably the more important part of a boy's participating in sports, as is learning to push himself to master a task. Boys universally, much more than girls, establish themselves in different ways in the pack of other boys through competition. It's always been this way. Our boys must be good, healthy competitors as well as know how to lose with grace and honor. Respect is traded man to man not so much by winning but by giving it your all and staying in the game to the end, having given the others a good run for their money.

All boys should be challenged to push themselves to the next level in some pursuit they show interest in. Dad, especially, should find healthy activities that fit his boy's personality. If he's more intellectual than physical, encourage him to pick a difficult book you think he will ultimately like and challenge him to hack his way through it, just as other boys might like hacking through a forest or a working on a difficult building project. My boy is a gifted painter and photographer, and he likes to skateboard and ride his bike. My job is to praise, affirm, and challenge him in these areas to help him be better than he was last month—all with great love and affirmation.

The mom and dad of every boy should be helping their son develop and construct a healthy and multifaceted vision of proper manhood that points the way to his own unique destination. There's no cookie-cutter formula for your boy, because he didn't come from a mold. The manhood journey that seems perfect for your friend's son can't be wholly copied and applied to your son, because God didn't give you your friend's boy. God gave you *your* son, and there is no other boy in the world like him. That is a great gift to you and the world. God and His world need your son to become the unique boy and man He created your boy to be!

As the project directors, you'll want to pay close attention both to the Creator of your boy and to your boy himself. Listen to both. Observe your son carefully. Talk long and often to both God and your boy with a listening heart. Help your son learn to recognize God's voice, to hear the direction He is giving to both of you about the kind of man He wants your son to be. Consulting the Designer and Manufacturer is a critical step in reaching the right destination of manhood.

Boys Must Recognize the Journey

Our sons must understand that if they are here and their destination of manhood lies there, then it will take a journey to get from here to there. This might seem obvious, but how many of our sons are intentionally on, engaged in, and moving through this journey? How many dads are walking with, leading, and talking their boys through it? How many moms are understanding and encouraging through the various stages, struggles, and successes? In God's timing, the journey is as important as the destination, because every moment that passes in our lives is a gift from God. These moments *are* the journey.

Yes, because of their own gender distinctions, moms and dads have different roles in guiding their sons on this journey. These roles relate to the parenting hearts and minds of mothers and fathers.

Mothers must understand that a boy needs to grow into a man. In doing so, he must face some challenges to develop the confidence and ability he needs to be a good man. This will conflict with your mothering heart. Every mother throughout time has had to face this tension. Jesus's mother certainly did, but she knew her Son had a larger calling and story. You will need to work out with your husband which challenges are appropriate for your boy. If dad wants to take your five-year-old boy whitewater rafting or get him his first chainsaw, you're right to insist he not do so. But if your husband wants to take your five-year-old on an overnight camping trip and you're uncomfortable with that, it's time to trust your husband.

Dads must appreciate that the journey sons are on is a process. This means he should only get to the right point at the right time. If you're on a road trip from Seattle to Miami, it's foolish to shoot for Graceland before you get to Denver. Take Denver as it comes, and you will make your way to Memphis in good time. The same holds true with your son's journey to manhood. He will get to the age where he can race motorcycles or go deep-sea fishing with you, if that's your thing. But you have to wait until he arrives.

For example, a twelve- or thirteen-year-old boy racing motorcycles can be a blast for the boy and his father. Doing so when Junior is seven or eight can be unwise and rightfully have mom freaked out. His time will come. Wait for and prepare him for it. Don't dump him in the deep end.

Finally, both moms and dads need to help their sons realize that the journey has to progress but not too fast. Our boys should know they will land at important markers along their wonderful journey into manhood; good moms and dads identify key progress points to anticipate and celebrate when their son reaches those places. The journey to manhood is the cumulative impact, influence, and experience of each critical step: learning to be a servant leader among his peers; helping protect others; delivering the goods and not giving up until the job is done; facing up to the truth and doing what's right; taking reasonable chances; making a difference; having a good influence on others and helping make them better; respecting women, elders, and peers; and all the other wonderful qualities that make a good man.

BOYS MUST NOT BE AFRAID TO BE MEN

Some people in our culture think that maleness is an illness that humanity must be cured of. This radical part of the feminist movement has had an unfortunate but substantial influence on men, leading us to view our masculinity as something to be overcome.

The sour fruit of this thinking is that men can be afraid to be men. I know I struggle with it. Is it polite or offensive to open a door for a woman? Is it polite or demeaning to offer to take boxes from the arms of female colleague as she carries them to her car or office? What about giving your umbrella to a woman? Are you saying she is a weaker creature, or are you honoring her?

G. K. Chesterton, known for his sharp wit, said he could never treat a woman as a peer; if he did she would roundly turn him out of the house because he would no doubt offend her. Indeed, women are the beings that cause men to act with civility and decorum. Women are why manners exist, and this is not a weakness of women. As we noted earlier, this points to the great power and influence that women hold.

Peggy Noonan, a presidential speechwriter during the early 1980s and now a celebrated author and commentator, tells the story of when she was a young woman in college, pumped up with feminist bravado and the high ideals of independence that were especially popular at the time. She was boarding a plane to go home for the holidays and was trying to put her carry-on luggage into the overhead bin. Seeing her struggle a bit, the gentleman in the seat behind her stood to offer his assistance. She shot him a look as if it were coming from the barrel of a gun; she told him she didn't need a man's help and she was quite capable herself. Today she is horrified by that youthful and rude display, recognizing that this kind man possibly never helped another woman again, and all because of her immaturity and insecurity.

Our boys should *never* be led to think that an act of gentlemanly kindness to a woman is anything but an act of kindness. They should be taught that such an act is a sign of respect, even if the woman doesn't receive it as such. A good man doesn't ask or require anyone's permission to be a gentleman! It's simply part of who he is. Good men treat women with care and respect, regardless of whether or not the woman is comfortable with her own femininity.

Our boys shouldn't be afraid to lead in a situation that requires leadership: to organize, direct, and fix, not with an attitude of superiority or power, but with one of humble graciousness and service. Nearly anyone can boss people around. Few people can lead and direct in such a way as to make others feel cared for and protected. Help your boy discern the difference between servant leadership and arrogance. Help him know which one demands more strength and character. Dad, point it out when you see this quality in other men, and seek to demonstrate it yourself.

Help your boy learn that he never needs to apologize for being a good man.

Boys Must Learn What a Good Husband Is

Amy and Leon Kass, distinguished professors at the University of Chicago, tell of an interesting and disturbing event that happened in one of their classes some years ago. When asked to describe the most important decision they would make in their lifetimes, many students mentioned deciding where they would do their graduate study, the kind of career they would enter, and where they would choose to live. After hearing many similar statements, one student confidently spoke up and said, "Deciding who should be the mother of my children!"[3]

His answer hit the class like a small bomb. The class broke into equal measures of laughter, eye rolling, and derision. Why? Some in the class assumed he was speaking of merely selecting a woman as a child-production unit. Others thought his answer as too traditional. The rest thought such a thing wasn't that important or would "just happen" at the right time.

But this young man knew what was really important. He knew that who he marries and enters into the life experience of parenting with matters tremendously. He spoke of being intentional about something most people think Cupid just brings along, like the stork delivers babies. He was right to identify this as his most important life decision. I hope that as a true man he wasn't moved by his classmates' reactions.

Nearly all men desire to marry. In fact, academic surveys reveal that having a happy marriage is consistently one of the top answers young men give as a major life goal, even above having a lot of money or a successful job.[4] No doubt one of your life dreams is for your boy to marry a wonderful woman; when he does, you'll have a happier son, you'll gain a sweet daughter-in-law, and you'll be one step closer to winning the jackpot of life—grandchildren.

If most men want to be married, is it strange or incorrect for moms and dads to recognize that today they are raising someone's future husband? Think about your own marriage relationship. What did the parents of the husband do right or wrong in raising a good man? If you think about the greatest emotional and character strengths or struggles of yourself and your spouse, they can probably be traced to something your respective parents did well or not so well.

My father taught me how to stick with something until it's done, to be honest and responsible. He taught me to work hard and not expect anyone to give me anything. He taught me to strike a healthy balance between work and spending time with my family, because that's what he did. However, he didn't teach me to be patient or to just roll with life with my wife and children. He didn't teach me that I can find strength and nobility in honoring my wife. In his defense, my father's dad didn't teach him much of anything, because he was hardly around and his mother died when he was a toddler. The point is that we inherit what we inherit. As dads, we try to pass on what is good and be sure that whatever is not good comes to the end of the line in us.

Of course, your son's life will consist of more than being a husband. But the skills, attitudes, and disciplines he learns during adolescence will serve him in many areas. Both moms and dads play a vital role in helping boys become good husbands.

For example, when we dads make mistakes, as good men we own them and seek to do better in front of our kids. When our boys and girls see this, it teaches strength of character and humility.

Children also learn from mom as she clearly and appropriately communicates what a wife needs and wants in a husband. This doesn't mean she has to agree with her husband on everything or that she must blindly accept his faults. Rather, her children need to see their mom and dad work through relational challenges in a healthy way.

Boys Must Learn What a Good Father Is

Just as nearly every young man wants to marry one day, the same research shows that just as many also want to have children, a family of their own. We help and encourage our boys to prepare for the workforce by doing well in school and for athletics by practicing their sport and getting better. But why don't we intentionally teach boys how to accomplish one of their greatest self-spoken life goals: becoming good fathers?

Many of us do, simply by being good fathers to our children and giving our boys a good example to follow. This is remarkably valuable. But setting a good example isn't the same as teaching our boys the specific skills, behaviors, attitudes, and knowledge they need to develop as they grow into men and eventually become dads. They need to learn that fathering is a valuable and noble calling. This takes place in at least three ways.

First, our boys must learn that fatherhood is not a status but rather an action and a vocation. The primary determiner of a dad's success or failure is whether or not he is there. He needs to show up to the job site to get the work done. Dad has to put in the hours with boots on the ground. He can't phone in. He can get a lot of things wrong and overcome his faults, but it's impossible to make up for the failure to be there. You might have a problem being harsh or impatient with your kids. But if you are involved in their lives, they get the message loud and clear that you care, even if you don't do it perfectly.

Second, our boys must learn that fatherhood is directive. Being a dad means mentoring, leading, and patient modeling. Truett Cathy, a very kind man and founder of the Chick-fil-A enterprise, says it is easier to build good men from the start than to fix bad men later. It's much easier when boys learn the qualities of a good father when they are young rather than needing to unlearn unhealthy behaviors, attitudes, and beliefs after they've become fathers.

Third, our boys (and girls) need to know that their father is crazy about and delights in them. A mom's love is often taken for granted because it's demonstrated daily in consistent and reliable ways. But a father's love carries an immeasurable impact, providing a strong source of confidence, personal acceptance, and empathic development in our children.

Our boys should learn that good fatherhood is an important and deeply rewarding life goal and a privilege they can look forward to enjoying.

Boys Must Learn How to Get It Done

As we discussed earlier, a man's nature is to see the job through. A good man cannot *not* finish the job and be at peace.

I'm in the middle of a huge backyard project of cleaning out the rock garden. One night several years ago, the topsoil of our neighbor's yard washed into the perimeter rocks of our yard during a Noah-like rainstorm. This created the perfect situation for all manner of weeds to grow from this part of our yard where no foliage is wanted. So I have to clear out all the rocks, wash the caked soil off each one, lay down new anti-weed fabric, and replace all the newly cleaned rocks. This has been a long, arduous, backbreaking process, and too many times I've tried to talk myself into *liking* the now weed-infested rock garden. But I know I must keep at it, making a little progress every month. I don't know when I'll finish, but I do know I will finish. And as long as I make good progress every so often, my manliness stays in good condition.

Think about this seeing-it-through quality and men. We know it was men who built the great pyramids in Egypt and Central and South America and the impressive Colosseum and other megacomplexes of ancient Rome. Men took on the transocean exploration voyages in the dawning age of world exploration and created the great skylines of emerging cities in the late 1800s and early 1900s. Men forged the Erie and Panama Canals, founded large corporations and manufacturing plants in the Industrial Age, and executed the space exploration program both by gazing into space with massive and powerful telescopes and by launching into space manned and unmanned spacecraft.

Men have a grand tradition of getting the job done, and our boys must learn the virtue and value of seeing a job through to the end. We help them learn this quality by giving our sons tasks to accomplish. At first, these tasks should fit their capabilities. As the years pass and our boys grow more skilled and confident, we should give them jobs just beyond their ability so they'll be challenged to figure how to complete the tasks. We also need to remember to let our sons try things their own way and make mistakes. If they don't have failing experiences from time to time to learn from, they won't learn well. What's more, they won't learn how to cope with failure when they are men. Mistakes are essential teachers, so don't deny your boy their benefit.

BOYS MUST LEARN WHEN TO SAY YES AND WHEN TO SAY NO

A boy starts to become a man when he begins to discern what opportunities and challenges he should say yes to and which he should say no to—and can explain his reasons for making such decisions. He will become a leader by articulating a clear rationale to others. He must also learn how to *act* on this knowledge, to the point where he instinctively says yes to the right things and no to the wrong things and when others can depend on him to do so.

Think about a time when you've seen an adult male act more like a boy than a man. Ask yourself if not responding correctly to the right and wrong things was a factor.

The movie *About a Boy,* based on a Nick Hornby novel, wonderfully illustrates the lighter side of this men-who-are-still-boys reality. The lonely, poor, and fatherless boy in the story comes to realize that he is more of a man than the wealthy man he has attached himself to. A key factor in this switching of roles is that the wealthy man had life easy, while the boy was toughened through sad and difficult circumstances. Ironically, the man learns from the boy how to step up and be a man.

A good man is a male who instinctively does the right thing at the right time for the right reasons. In this way, we shouldn't be afraid to tell our eight-year-old boy that he acted like a man today when he did the right thing at the right time. He needs to hear it.

Boys Must Learn to Take Control
at the Right Time

September 11, 2001, stands as a watershed moment in American history. At that moment, manliness came back into fashion, at least for a while. Think of President Bush and how things changed dramatically for him and our nation in a moment.

The contrast of *before* and *after* is quite stark. The leader of the free world was sitting in an inner-city second-grade classroom reading a story titled "The Pet Goat" to a circle of children. Pretty mundane stuff, not what most people would think of as manly. Then his chief of staff, Andrew Card, stepped up to the president and whispered something in his ear. The expression on President Bush's face changed immediately. Recently I was talking to a friend who worked in the Bush White House close to the president, and I described to him my impression of the president's thinking at that moment, based on video footage I've seen.

As Andrew Card walks over and speaks into the president's ear, you see not so much a look of surprise as one of "Okay, so this is how this is going down!" knowing that national security reports of al Qaeda attacks were circulating. And immediately, the president tilts his head back a bit and starts to think of his proper response. He stays in his seat with the children because he doesn't want to express alarm. With the cameras on him, he thinks it best to quickly but calmly finish what he's doing and then determine what's going wrong. But his first look is one of anger tempered by strong resolve and control.

My friend said my description was exactly right. He explained that one of the most amazing experiences of his life was watching President Bush respond to having this herculean weight suddenly placed on his shoulders. He was struck by the president's moral resolve, strength, conviction, and calm. Even his critics agree that the president showed remarkable leadership throughout that day and the following weeks, regardless of their particular thoughts about his execution and management of the wars that followed.

New York City mayor Rudy Giuliani also showed the right kind of control at the right time during the aftermath of the 9/11 attacks. He was clearly shaken by the experience, yet he led with boldness, confidence, and a tender heart. He attended every funeral of every fallen public servant employed by the city. He was strong and he cried with others.

This is what men do, and it gives comfort to all around.

In contrast, think of the way Bruce Ismay was portrayed in *Titanic*, James Cameron's 1997 film. In the movie, this high-ranking representative of the White Start Line, the ship's maker, was consumed with concern that both his own reputation and that of the "unsinkable" ship would be ruined. His self-absorption prevented him from giving the captain accurate advice or making decisions that would've saved hundreds of passengers. Instead he saved himself by sneaking into a lifeboat dressed as a woman. He did not act like a man.[5]

Good men know when a situation calls for them to take control, and they don't shrink from what needs to be done.

Boys Must Learn Self-Sacrifice

Choosing selflessness is what separates the men from the boys. Men are willing to sacrifice themselves for the good of others. Nearly all the qualities our boys need to learn in their journey into manhood are tied up in this characteristic.

Good husbands and fathers are men who sacrifice for their wives and children. Speaking of the *Titanic*, what did those who watched the movie think of the men who tricked or pushed their way into the limited and overcrowded rescue boats? In reality, it's recorded that the captain of the ship shouted to the crew to "Be British!" This was understood by all the men—not just the crew—that the men should stay calm and let seats in the lifeboats go to the women and children. If this manly quality of self-sacrifice were just a social construct or merely a quality of "being British," then some people in the various countries where the film played would see these cheating and selfish men as shrewd, simply taking care of themselves. But do you think any man or woman who saw the movie anywhere in the world excused the men who forced their way into the rescue boats and took the place of the women and children? These men were seen by all as selfish cowards because it is universally understood that good men sacrifice themselves for others.

Our boys might not ever be called to give up their seats on a lifeboat. They might never be required to perform other heroic acts like throwing themselves on a live grenade or dismantling a bomb. But the orientation toward sacrificing selfish concerns in day-in and day-out human interactions is a masculine attitude and quality that our boys must learn. In becoming selfless men, they give to those around them a sense of comfort, security, and confidence that they are in good hands.

STEERING BOYS TOWARD MANHOOD

This isn't an exhaustive list of what boys must learn on their way to becoming good men, but these are some of the most important qualities.

- Boys must recognize the destination.
- Boys must recognize the journey.
- Boys must not be afraid to be or apologize for being men.
- Boys must learn what a good husband is.
- Boys must learn what a good father is.
- Boys must learn how to get it done.
- Boys must learn when to say yes and when to say no.
- Boys must learn to take control at the right time.
- Boys must learn self-sacrifice.

It's a good and healthy exercise for you as mom and dad to talk about this list together as well as with your son, to see if there are others that apply. What would your son add? This would depend on your boy's personality, gifting, and calling as well as the calling of your family. A young Sam Walton, Martin Luther King Jr., or Billy Graham will have special callings as men that your son might not have and vice versa.

As we discussed, adolescence is key in taking our boys from boyhood to manhood. Simple physics explains why it's easier to steer a great ship when it's moving than when it's standing still. The same is true for males. Adolescence is the period in a boy's life where he is best steered into manhood, because the changes going through his mind, body, and spirit are propelling him toward adulthood. This is where the real molding into manhood happens, and both mother and father play key roles here.

Remember, mom's role is to be the pusher toward manhood. A boy has a very special and close bond with mom. Mom is and has likely been his primary source of security and comfort. Given this, she should be the one to gently *push* her son toward putting away childish boy things and moving toward manhood. Because our boys need so much to have dad's affirmation and acceptance, dad's role is to *draw* boys—to invite them—into manhood. Mom is the stick; dad is the carrot. Together, in different but necessary ways, moms and dads move boys along this conveyer belt to male maturity and identity, the good place called manhood.

Our boys have great and essential needs on their road to manhood. The boys who have those needs met well are truly blessed and prepared for life. Their wives and children are blessed as well. The boys who don't get these needs met will have greater and deeper struggles, as will their wives and children.

What kind of story will your child tell of his growing years? What kind of man are you and your spouse working to create for his wife and children?

As anthropologist Margaret Mead learned from her study, the nurturing husband and parenting behaviors of men must be learned. Mothers and fathers are the best and wisest teachers. God has given parents this grand honor and profound challenge. Nothing of such consequence is easy, nor should it be entered into lightly. But the reward is like nothing else in life.

You are in the business of making men. Seize it!

How do my husband and I help our teenage son learn not to be afraid of being a man but also keep him from being macho and arrogant?

If I understand your question correctly, you are asking about helping your boy unapologetically become a man and do what good men do without concern for the judgment of others, yet not become a walking cartoon of masculinity.

Becoming a good man comes down to a few key qualities: service, protection, and respect. If any man takes control of a situation or helps another person and does so in the spirit of service, protection, and respect, he never needs to apologize. A good man doesn't need to convince people of his strength. He demonstrates it by what he does: helping, protecting, leading, serving, honoring, showing concern for others. He also demonstrates his strength by what he doesn't do: intimidate for no reason, brag, put people down, or use violence or force for his first course of action.

When you say boys should learn what a good husband and father is, isn't that rushing the game? Shouldn't that come later, like maybe in their twenties?

Interestingly, the age of first marriage has been rising for both men and women. In fact, it's approaching just under thirty years of age for both, with women typically just a bit younger than men on the wedding day.[6] This means that young adults are entering into marriage after living on their own for longer periods of time than their parents and grandparents.

As a result, they are more set in their ways in terms of their life routine: how they live life and manage finances, careers, and free time. This makes it harder for two such "set" lives to merge in marriage.

Also, marriage becomes one of the central relationships of adult life for the overwhelming majority of men and women. Our children want to succeed at and find happiness in marriage. As parents, of course, you desire the same thing for your children. Why then does it seem strange to prepare our sons to understand how to be good husbands and fathers— something they deeply desire? It's highly likely their life roads will go in that direction; a good man anticipates what lies ahead on the journey and prepares for it.

We should be preparing our boys to take on the responsibilities and joys of marriage and family life. Good husbands and fathers don't just happen; we have to create them.

SIX

Metamorphosis to Womanhood: Making Healthy Women out of Healthy Girls

I asked my fifth grader, Tess, what girls like her needed most to become good women. She is at that stage where she's learning to become a young woman, slowly leaving behind her little-girl behaviors and habits.

She knew exactly what the answer was: "Easy, Daddy. The most important thing a woman needs is to have great hair and to smell good."

So there you go! Take it from Tess.

Later I asked the same question of my thirteen-year-old daughter, Sophie. Her answer was just as immediate: the only thing a girl really needs to be a good woman is lip gloss.

Great hair, good smell, and lip gloss. Mom and dad, how hard is that? And they say women are more complex than men.

The Complexity of a Woman

I wish that I could say that helping a girl become a healthy woman was as easy as that. But as bright as my daughters are, I think well-rounded and healthy femininity is a bit more complex.

We should appreciate what a profound life transition takes place when a girl becomes a woman. I'm amazed that my oldest daughter, Olivia, is sixteen, one year *older* than Jackie was when I met her thirty years ago and we started our relationship in earnest. But of course, my wife-to-be seemed so much older then than my daughter does now.

A good woman is the more intricate of the species, for while both men and women are complex and profound, women universally have more interesting layers to their femininity than men have to their masculinity. You only have to look at how women and men adorn themselves when going out among their community or what materials they use to give character to their living spaces. Our girls should take pride in their more complicated selves.

As parents guide their girls into the complex and wonderful world of healthy womanhood, what do they need to be aware of?

What are the essential qualities that transform our daughters into mature, secure women?

As you read through the qualities described below, please keep in mind that much of this is innate, but because our culture seems to fight so hard to suppress certain natural tendencies, it's our privilege and responsibility as parents to watch for opportunities to nurture and guide in these areas. Again, this list isn't exhaustive, because that would be impossible given the mystery and depth of the two sexes as specifically unique statues of who God is in the world. Such an essence and being can never be fully contained or explained. No doubt, you'll be able to add more from your experience and insights, and I encourage you to think about what those could be.

GIRLS NEED TO BE AWARE OF THEIR POWER

The greatest thing we can help our girls understand as they grow into women is how powerful womanhood is. I don't mean this as some hollow "I am woman, hear me roar!" pep talk. If you have to explain to people how strong you are, then you're actually not very powerful.

Think about Mary Gates and the young man she unleashed upon the world. In fact, something called the Mother's Club at young Bill Gates's exclusive prep school organized a rummage sale to raise money to purchase the hardware that gave students access to an early computer. On this computer young Bill created his first computer program, a tic-tac-toe game that students could play. That simple game led to numerous other developments that had major impact on our world today—all because of one mom and a school's seemingly inconsequential group for mothers.

Power comes in some of the most unlikely places. As the intellectual George Gilder explains,

> Women control not the economy of the marketplace but the
> economy of eros: the life force in our society and our lives. What
> happens in the inner realm of women finally shapes what happens
> on our social surfaces, determining the level of happiness, energy,
> creativity, morality, and solidarity in the nation.[1]

Women can be immeasurably powerful by simply being good, healthy women. Such women can't help but shape, mold, influence, and direct their environments at home, school, work, community, church, and everywhere else they go. Men take control and lead, but women influence.

Women also have power in that every new person who comes into the world—including those who have had a profound mark on history—came from this being called woman. Think about anyone who you believe has rocked the world for the good. He or she could not have done that if it weren't for a woman called mom. A woman allowed George Washington to become the father of a great nation. A woman allowed Abraham Lincoln to keep that nation together with his moral and political skill. A woman allowed the Reverend Martin Luther King Jr. to lead us to a better place. Women allowed Emily Dickinson to give us amazing poetry and Jane Austen to give us beautiful literature. Vincent van Gogh's mom made our lives better. Think of anything consequential that has come to life through human creativity—in the arts, religion, industry, the sciences, politics, culture, law—and a woman made it possible.

Women wield power and influence simply by being women in the world. Think of the women who impact your workplace, your child's school, your city government, the places you shop, the universities you attended, as well as the arts you enjoy. They shape each of these places as they think, act, influence, lead, challenge, and serve as women.

As our girls mature into women, they must learn to recognize, appreciate, and use the God-given feminine power of a woman.

GIRLS NEED TO BE ENCOURAGED
TO TAKE PRIDE IN THEIR SOFT STRENGTH

Most healthy and secure women tend to think that describing another woman as "strong" or having "a strong personality" is a negative statement. The term *strong* carries a connotation that the woman has some insecurity she is trying to cover or make up for. I'm not sure these assumptions are fair, but they are what they are.

Fair or not, a woman is strongest and most influential when her strength is "soft." Think about a highly skilled female schoolteacher. It's likely that her control of her class comes most often not from demonstrations of power or threats of punishment but from a quiet tip of her head, a raise of an eyebrow, or simply getting quiet and making eye contact with the students.

I remember this being remarkably effective during my school years. If the class got excited and out of control, the good teacher just needed to stop talking for thirty seconds to bring the unruly class to silence. In fifth grade I had my first male teacher. Any student who talked out of turn or disrupted the class was called forward for a good whack on the palm of the hand with his heavy ruler. Men exert physical assertiveness, even if through a commanding voice, to get control. Women are more likely to do "nothing" yet somehow command order out of chaos. That's power.

Consider a female character in a recent movie who through her gentle strength transforms a hardened, angry man. In *Gran Torino*, Sue Lor, a teenage girl from the multigenerational Hmong family next door, meets the cold, offensive, and bitter Walt Kowalski, played by Clint Eastwood. She alone is responsible for getting this hard-baked man to open up to and be accepted by her family. She accomplishes this by gently pushing back on Walt's consistently rude efforts to keep anyone from getting close to him. He comes to respect Sue because she isn't intimidated and won't give up on being gracious toward him. This young girl has remarkable power and knows how use it.

As our girls move toward becoming confident and healthy women, we must help them understand that their natural inclination toward soft strength is a deep and powerful gift of womanhood. They certainly don't need to be ashamed of this gift; in fact, they can take pride in using it well, for the betterment of others.

GIRLS NEED TO LEARN
TO BE CONFIDENT IN THEIR FEMININITY

As young women, our daughters should learn that they have nothing to prove. A healthy woman seldom brings attention to her femininity. It's simply part of her innate nature, and people never doubt it.

I find Oprah Winfrey to be a good example of this. She is a remarkably influential woman. But she is also soft and feminine and very confident in her power. On her show, even when she is setting someone straight with all the confidence in the world, she is soft in doing so. Yet no one believes the recipient gets off easy. In contrast, my impression of Whoopi Goldberg is that she lacks this kind of confidence. She seems to feel a need to remind people that she's someone to be reckoned with. Sometimes she seems to be trying to overcome her femininity. Which of the two is the more powerful, healthy, influential woman?

Think of the strongest, well-balanced woman you know, and consider how she carries and presents her femininity. There are as many different ways to do this as there are women, but clearly some are healthier and more secure than others.

Look at the world of music to see how various women express their femininity in very different ways: Odetta, Natalie Merchant, Alicia Keys, Annie Lennox, Lucinda Williams, Faith Hill, Patty Griffin, Carole King, Aretha Franklin, Bonnie Raitt, Cyndi Lauper, and Dolores O'Riordan. Each of these women is thoroughly feminine in very different ways, but each is appreciated as a woman.

As our girls develop into women, they must understand that femininity is a very real and specific human quality that they can demonstrate in a variety of ways and still be solidly feminine. One of the biggest false assumptions we make about femininity is that it looks exactly like *this* or *that*. Rather, femininity is the artful coming together of many factors, and every truly feminine woman puts those together in wonderfully different ways. The result is healthy women who are comfortable and confident in the femininity they present to the world.

Just as a healthy woman doesn't need to announce or actively bring attention to her femininity, she doesn't apologize for it either. She is who she is.

Are you familiar with the Victorian novelist George Eliot? George was actually Mary Anne Evans, a woman whose husband was named George. She presented herself publicly as a male author so she could ensure her work would be taken seriously. But has anybody really thought that two of her key female influences, Charlotte Brontë and Jane Austen, were not serious writers and thinkers? Evans, who suffered from low self-confidence, was essentially apologizing for being feminine.

One of my family's favorite painters, Mary Cassatt, was the one woman who broke into the fraternity of impressionist painters. She did so by painting women as mothers caring for their babies and children. She was who she was. Cassatt, along with so many other good women in history, said with her life, essentially, "I will not be anyone other than who I am, and if you can't accept me, you will be the poorer for it!"

Girls Need to Be Encouraged to Revel in Their Unique Human Design

Now this might not seem like something we need to impress on our girls as they move toward womanhood. Yet bearing children is fundamental to being a woman, and girls should appreciate the gift of fertility in age-appropriate ways.

Too many women have been taught to see their fertility as a weakness. This is exactly why legal abortion is nearly a sacrament to radical feminists. They believe that if a woman can't become unpregnant at will, she is disadvantaged. However, this is a deeply antiwoman attitude because it suggests that a certain natural aspect of being a woman is a condition that needs fixing. A woman doesn't get pregnant because something went wrong; rather, her womanhood went quite right.

In bearing a child, a woman does something that only she and God can do. No other being in the universe can do it. She has the ability to bring forth new God-imagers into the world. Why should she ever apologize for this amazing power?

As girls become women, they must learn to respect and glory in the miracle of a woman's calling and ability as a life giver. Her ability to give life extends into her deep desire to nurture that new life. A healthy woman doesn't see this as weakness, and a well-balanced woman never apologizes for it. She revels in it, and her family rejoices along with her.

Girls Need to Learn the Value of Relationships

Men are very much defined by their work. When men meet, they commonly ask, "How's work going?" When a man isn't working, he often feels incomplete, as though he's not pulling his share of the load. Women are different. Of course, they can find their work extremely rewarding and important, both to themselves and their community. But they seldom value themselves in relation to their work.

A woman's contentment in life comes largely from her circle of friends, her husband, her parents, and her children—not necessarily in that order. In other words, she finds her contentment in her relationships. Often, the satisfaction she finds in her work is more connected to the rewarding relationships she gains through her work rather than a sense of accomplishment about the work. She derives more pleasure from these relationships, and it bothers her more deeply when problems arise in these friendships.

Jackie and I have a good friend who was a successful and highly placed CPA for a large firm. When she had kids, her babies happily and naturally became her full-time work. But she still goes and meets with the women she worked with many years ago. She misses her career from time to time, which prompted her to volunteer her professional talents with a nearby ministry. But she misses the friendships she had at work far more. Although many of the other women she worked with are now full-time moms as well, they have all kept up their relationships.

Anthropologists find this relational nature is true of women around the world and across diverse cultures, as women often arrange to do their daily work in the community of other women. The quilting circle is not merely a feminine colonial rarity. As our girls become women, they should recognize and appreciate the special value women place on their relationships.

GIRLS NEED TO KNOW THEY CAN CALL OUT THE BEST IN OTHERS

Jackie and I try to watch the movie *As Good as It Gets* at least once a year. Melvin Udall (Jack Nicholson) is a deeply obsessive-compulsive and narcissistic writer who slowly falls in love with the only waitress in his regular restaurant who has the patience to deal with his rudeness and quirkiness. She is a confident and attractive young single mother, Carol Connelly (Helen Hunt). Even as they grow closer, he is helpless to keep from insulting her regularly.

In one scene, they find themselves out for a nice evening at a fancy restaurant. When Melvin criticizes Carol's dress, she tells him he has no idea how much his words hurt her and that he'd better come up with a compliment pretty quick. She even reminds him that a compliment is something nice that one person says to another.

Melvin thinks for a long, anxious minute, then announces, "I've got a really great compliment for you, and it's true." Her body language indicates fear that he probably couldn't tell a good compliment from an insult and wonders what's coming. After an awkward, rambling lead-in, Melvin finally says, "You make me want to be a better man."

Carol's look is one of bewilderment. When watching the movie, you don't know if her surprise is good or bad and how she's going to react. She finally says quietly, "That's maybe the best compliment of my life."

And Melvin responds, "Well, maybe I overshot a little, because I was aiming at just enough to keep you from walking out."

Carol laughs. At this moment Carol realizes she has the power of womanhood to change a man. And she knows changing this particular one is pretty heavy lifting. Melvin realizes this also. She knows what the compliment says about her, and it takes her breath away. Melvin finally spoke to her as a woman.

Most of us know at least one good woman who's in a relationship with a man who is obviously bad for her. She seems way too centered and smart, but there she goes, jumping heart first into the deep end of this relationship, believing she can fix him. In fact, as a woman, she needs to try to fix him. Women in good relationships have the same power— power to entice and inspire their men to want to be better men.

This influence of a woman is a mystery of humanity and one key reason why every culture at every time in every populated place on the earth has marriage in some form, where men are permanently connected to women and vice versa. Over time, every culture has found that married men become better citizens. The impact a woman has on a man is not a cultural construct but a human truism.

Girls Need to Learn How to Care for Others

A woman's nature, for the most part, is to be inclusive, welcoming, and warm. If a room of people are talking and enjoying one another's company and a new couple enters seeming too reserved or shy to get into the mix, someone will typically break from the crowd and welcome the newcomers. Most likely, that someone will be a woman. She is more sensitive to the feelings, hurts, fears, and concerns of others. She's more perceptive of and responsive to the nonverbal cues of those around her. She is likely to delve into the lives and feelings of people, making sure that all is well or seeing how she can help.

As our girls move toward becoming women, they should understand that this caring, making of friends, and showing inclusiveness is natural and proper. Of course, our daughters should understand that there are parameters to these feminine qualities; they can make our girls dangerously vulnerable, physically and emotionally. They must also learn when their involvement is helpful and welcome and when it's not. In addition, they need to grasp that although helping and caring for others is a positive characteristic of strength, they must blend compassion with discernment.

Girls Need to Be Encouraged to Value Their Personal Sense of Beauty

Picture a single twenty-two-year-old man's apartment. Think about the layout of his living room. Imagine what he might have hanging on the walls. Think about how the different items—couches and chairs, tables and lighting, accessories—interact with one another designwise. Now imagine a single twenty-two-year-old woman's apartment in all the same ways. Would they be different from each other? In what ways?

If you believe there would be no real difference at all, let me ask you, if either apartment was offered to you for a week in a city of your choice, whose apartment would be most enjoyable to stay in—the young man's or young woman's?

Women are naturally more attuned to beauty in design, clothing, and art as well as in literature and movies. They are more likely to bring beauty to any setting they come to for any significant period of time. This is one way women connect with and influence their environments, and the results are appreciated by all.

Women don't dress more attractively than men because they are required to. No law says that women have to accessorize like they do. They do it because they desire to. My girls love to go to Claire's and can spend an hour looking at all the little accessories for their hair and nails, the bracelets and necklaces, and all the other girly goodies. No one had to tell them they should like such things; their mom and I didn't have to work hard to carefully develop these interests in them.

A woman's eyes, mind, and heart gravitate more naturally toward beauty than a man's. Yes, a man can recognize the beauty of a sunset over the Rocky Mountains, the green pastures of Ireland, or the azure waters of the Caribbean. But such observations don't take much skill or attentiveness. Women, however, are more likely to notice the colors, textures, layout, and accents of every room they enter. They are also more likely to make immediate conclusions about what works in the room and what doesn't as well as what they might do with it if it were theirs. These distinctions about beauty aren't true of every woman and man. But recognizing and bringing beauty to the world is more often a quality of women than of men, and it's largely universal.

As our daughters become women, they should appreciate this virtue in themselves and the other women around them. All of us should value the presence of this quality in the women in our lives because we all benefit from it.

Girls Need to Be Affirmed
in Their Search for Security

A good woman not only desires security and safety, she insists on it. She doesn't apologize for wanting to be secure, because her expectation is not a weakness but part of her strength. As we touched on earlier, a woman's whole biological orientation is to take in life, to provide warmth and security for it, and to create a safe and nurturing place to thrive. Her body, her nature, her desire, her *womanness* is pointed toward safety and security. She can't *not* be this way!

Therefore, it's natural for her to live out this expectation in everyday life: to want her house properly secured, to take the safest route to where she is going, and to avoid unsafe people and the more dangerous parts of town. Jackie is more reticent about getting out and driving in the snow and ice we get in Colorado. I love it—the challenge, the slipping, the sliding, the unpredictability, the possibility of losing it. It doesn't make sense, but I'm a guy. At the same time I sometimes realize that Jackie's caution is often more healthy and wise than my desire for excitement.

As our girls mature into women, it is important that they understand that their need for safety and security isn't a quirk or a weakness; rather, it's a valuable part of their inherent femaleness. They need to see that good men honor the women in their lives by recognizing this expectation and providing it. The result is that this quality also keeps men safer.

Girls Need to Learn How
to Quietly Demand Respect

One of the indisputable differences between men and women centers on the issue of respect. While men need to earn respect in the community, a good woman expects it. When a man comes into a new group of men—in the workplace, on the sports field, at church—he is compelled to show that he's worthy of the group. The other men in the group will make a hundred different evaluations and measurements of him, mostly subconsciously, to size him up.

For women, the process is much different. Respect is largely hers to lose. A healthy woman walks into a new situation wearing the soft aroma of "I expect you to honor my womanliness."

Women honor this in one another by being gracious, welcoming, and affirming to the other women around them. A woman protects her own respect by respecting the other women around her, complimenting them, lifting them up, and drawing them in. A healthy woman will keep the respect of other women (and men) by always having something kind to say about any woman. If a particular woman isn't virtuous, a healthy woman responds with the treatment such a woman deserves: silence. Silence is a statement in itself and often a very proper response, as Proverbs teaches us over and over again.

As your daughter becomes a woman, you can help her recognize this expectation of respect in other women. You can help her practice it with her friends. Notice and study women who demonstrate this "expect respect" quality in healthy feminine ways. I have mentioned Rosa Parks a few times in these pages. She is a strong example in this regard. Talk about how your daughter might demonstrate the same quality in particular situations. At the same time, take note of women who seem to always be demanding respect in less secure and confident ways. Talk (discreetly) about what makes this unattractive in women. What makes these women less desirable to spend time with?

May I offer a gentle reminder? It's important to talk frequently about these principles and qualities to our children. Making note of those qualities when you see them demonstrated by others is often much more powerful and instructive. Fortunately, plenty of examples exist all around us:

in the people we see every day as well as in characters from movies and literature. The people we encounter in daily life provide living examples and memorable lessons in the attitudes, beliefs, and behaviors that are desirable and beautiful. But we should always look for and take note of these qualities with humility as students of life, never with a spirit of superiority or judgment.

Guiding Girls Toward Womanhood

Once again, this certainly isn't an exhaustive list of qualities of healthy, secure women. However, this list can serve as a helpful discussion starter for you and your daughter while she travels her own road toward becoming a woman. Some of the qualities will be truer of your daughter than others. Remember, your daughter is a God-created being who is new and unique to the world and human history. Your job is to help her become the special feminine creature that God created her to be. The wonder of your daughter as she becomes a woman will be found in these truths:

- Girls are powerful.
- Girls have soft strength.
- Girls are confident in their femininity.
- Girls revel in their unique design.
- Girls value relationships.
- Girls call out the best in others.
- Girls care for others.
- Girls recognize and bring beauty.
- Girls expect security.
- Girls quietly demand respect.

Urge your daughter to make a list of the qualities she believes are essential and desirable for her as she moves into womanhood. Remind her that her list can't be wrong, because God has given her a unique personality. This task should take one or more thoughtful and prayerful weeks. She might talk with her best, spiritually attuned friends for their perspective on her one-of-a-kind womanly design.

Go over her list with her when she is done, asking why she chose certain qualities and encouraging her to explain her thoughts to you. Take her seriously, and refrain from giving your opinions at this point. You can do that later in more natural discussions. Part of growing up into a secure young woman is experiencing the confidence others place in your choices and decisions. The confidence of parents is especially important.

Encourage your daughter to keep this list in a special place she can consult each year, maybe on her birthday or at the start of every school year, so she can assess how she is doing with each quality. What might she want to add to the list as she matures? Which items would she take off the list as the years pass?

Wouldn't it be fun for her to have this list to discuss with her own daughter when she gets to this age? If your mom had done something like this with you at the anxious adolescent stage of life, how much better would you have understood your own mother and your own transformation into womanhood?

—

One thing you didn't mention was helping our girls know what is appropriate clothing and style for a woman. Can you give some advice about guiding our daughters in this area?

Your first step is deciding what's important and what's not—the majors and the minors. If God has a favorite style of clothing, He didn't reveal it to us. However, this doesn't stop some believers from assuming they know exactly what style that is. Curiously, it's the same style they adopt, almost like a uniform. You know these people. This attitude can amount to a false spirituality or morality. Remember, Jesus's enemies were the ones who made a big deal about the smallest details. So don't assume that getting caught up in that makes you any closer or pleasing to God. God looks at the inside (see Matthew 23:25–26). So, here are two main questions we can ask regarding our daughters' clothing:

1. *Are your clothes modest and appropriate?* Are the clothes modest in that they accentuate your daughter's body in ways that are healthy and honoring? As they grow older, our daughters need to be aware that their clothes make statements about themselves, for good and bad, and that boys will have different reactions to their clothes than their girlfriends will.

2. *Are your clothes honoring to your womanhood?* Your daughters should always ask, "What am I trying to accomplish by wearing this? What impact do I want to have on others?" Then ask if that impact is appropriate in terms of modesty or the situation. Does it send the right message about her glory as a woman? Does it enhance this glory or diminish it?

As with all other issues touching on morality and style, our daughters (as well as our sons) must learn to make good judgments on their own, rather than always relying on mom and dad to tell them what to do. Our girls need to learn proper modesty and style for themselves. They need to grasp that being mindful of how they dress demonstrates esteem for themselves and others. Our clothing choices are like our visual manners to those around us.

Your daughter doesn't necessarily need to be a clone of mom. Help her develop the style and manner that suits her personality but does so in a way that speaks to her feminine dignity.

My daughter says most of the boys in her school are so timid that they seldom ask any of the girls out. She wants to ask a particular boy that she likes to go do something together one weekend. What do you think about girls asking boys out?

I'm not really a fan of this practice. Girls have always had their ways of communicating their interest to a particular young man. Often, the more subtly a girl does this, the better it speaks of her power. This keeps the girl from needing to be too forward, which comes off as desperate rather than classy. The boy should be sharp and bold enough to pick up on her cues. Besides, how many of us want our daughter to develop a relationship with a boy who isn't willing or doesn't have the confidence to invite her to spend time together? Such a boy needs to learn to step up. A woman has the power to send the message, "I might be interested in you, but I want to see how well you approach me."

Girls need to make up their minds about who they are and the value they place in themselves. They should both expect and require boys who are interested in them to start acting like young men if they want a shot at these girls' attention. This is how strong and confident women carry themselves. They don't need to beg for men. Women are most attractive in their feminine mystery.

PART II

Why Boys and Girls Need *Mothers* and *Fathers*

—

SEVEN

Why It's Good When Mom and Dad Disagree

Death and taxes are not the only sure things—not even the first sure things. Long before you ever gave the slightest concern about either, two things were absolutely certain about you:

1. You are the child of two people. Your very existence required a significant contribution from both a male and a female.
2. You arrived on the scene in the image of one of these. You are either male or female, like your mother or father.

These two things are certain, regardless of the uniqueness of your story or how much you like to color outside the lines. A recent cartoon in the *New Yorker* illuminates what I'm saying. A high-powered business-man is sitting in his office, speaking to a guest. On his desk are three small framed photographs, presumably of his children and one larger one of his wife. The caption says, "Yes, we were blessed with one of each!"

Give it a moment. You'll get it.

So many times, cartoons in the *New Yorker* are funny because they make note of the obvious in unusual ways. In this case, if the gender-spectrum movement—which claims that humanity consists of a full rainbow of genders—is correct, then this cartoon wouldn't be funny. In fact, only three wouldn't come close to covering it. The truth is that we only have two options. As parents, you've had the great joy of bringing others into this special club called humanity. If that's true of you, another thing is sure: *you didn't do it alone.* You needed help from a member of the other team, your co-parent from the other side of this street called humanity.

Regardless of how fancy we get with reproductive technology, males still need females and females still need males for the important task of bringing along the next generation of humanity. This mutual need is as absolute as gravity. It's one of the ways God gets us to cooperate.

While male and female not only bring very different and necessary things to the creation of each new human life, they also bring different and necessary things to the task of raising each new life to healthy, secure, and well-adjusted maturity. Sure as death and taxes. While the first *pro-creative* fact might seem as elementary as the birds and bees, this second *developmental* fact isn't as popularly known or appreciated. But both are vitally important because they explain *you*. They explain your spouse. And they are currently contributing to the stories that are your children.

This chapter, as well as the rest of the book, takes the differences between male and female we've already discussed in the context of your children and explores how those same differences in mom and dad contribute to the development of a child's health, security, compassion, confidence, intellect, and maturity. The many ways these differences affect healthy child development aren't widely understood or appreciated today. Yet every parent experiences these male-female parenting differences nearly every day, whether or not they realize it. Every child is influenced by them.

In my fifteen-year career as a full-time researcher on parenting and family issues, and in reading the countless books my wife and I have digested while raising our five children, I have not come across a book that explains these important mother-father differences and how they complement each other.[1]

Bridging the Gap

We often think our differences push us apart. But the natural and God-given differences between men and women can actually draw us closer as together we each uniquely contribute to our child's development.

But the differing ways you and your spouse parent will cause conflict between you as well. In my own marriage, too often I want Jackie to act more like me, and Jackie wants me to act more like her. We both tend to think our own approach to parenting issues is the right one. I'm sure this is also true of you and your spouse.

A few years ago, our twins, Sophie and Schaeffer, asked if they could go down to the rope swing with Ashley and Matthew, their friends from across the street. I thought it would be a great idea. Jackie did not! You see, the rope swing is down a hill from our house, around the corner, and hanging from a large oak tree that reaches out over a huge washed-out gulley. The gulley runs along a fairly busy roadway. (I know...I can hear moms saying, "What part of this looks safe?")

Jackie took all these things into consideration and told the twins, "Sorry, I don't think so." I took all these things into consideration and said, "It would be a good opportunity for the kids to show themselves responsible, especially going with the neighbor kids who have equally good judgment." We both noted the same issues, but Jackie saw the opportunity for safety and I saw the opportunity for personal growth and responsibility.

I yielded to Jackie's conclusion. But there are times when I need not yield as quickly and instead make a case for letting the kids go a bit beyond the boundaries we've set for them. This is what marriage and parenting are all about—negotiating so that each parent's concerns are heard and providing the kids with opportunities to grow and expand their worlds as safely as possible.

Do you deal with this struggle in your marriage? If so, I hope the information in the following chapters can help you recognize and negotiate the inevitable conflicts in a healthier way and see these differences as a part of nature—and important to your child's development—rather than merely a stubborn stand by your spouse.

Mom, have you ever wondered, *Why does he always let the kids ride their bikes in the street?* or, *Why is he letting my baby climb so high up in that tree?*

Dad, do you wonder, *Why does she excuse the kids' behavior when they break the rules?* or, *How are our children going to learn to solve problems for themselves if she is always there to solve things for them?*

The mother way and father way of parenting—which sometimes seem incomprehensible and simply wrongheaded to our spouse—create necessary opportunities for growth and healthy development in our children. And they have for millenniums. The answer to good parenting is to help men see how, as men, they uniquely contribute essential qualities that their children need, to help women see how, as women, they contribute essential qualities that their children need, and for each parent to recognize and appreciate the contributions of the other.

I've been speaking on this topic for many years in all regions of the country to parents of all socioeconomic circumstances. What makes these talks fun for me and the audience is how mothers and fathers elbow each other throughout the presentation and flash a look as if to say, "See, that's why I do that, and it's good for our child!" Even though these moms and dads have studied very little child-development theory, they live it and readily recognize these truths in their own families when pointed out to them.

Mothers and fathers will come up with their spouses in tow after I speak and playfully ask me to reiterate a particular point—just to make sure it was understood by the other parent. We all have a good laugh. You can see the happiness on their faces as someone finally acknowledges the wisdom behind something their spouse finds to be senseless! It's true for both husbands and wives.

This discovery helps couples more peaceably understand and bridge the dad-mom parenting divide—a divide that is fundamental and necessary to shaping our children into healthy adults. I pray you learn something important about your divine role as a sex-distinct God-imager in your marriage, particularly as your child's parent. Missing this would mean cheating yourself, your child, and the larger community that needs healthy, well-adjusted, and productive people.

WHAT BABIES KNOW ABOUT THE DIFFERENCES BETWEEN MOM AND DAD

When Jackie was first pregnant, I wished so badly for the "good old days" when fathers were relegated to a waiting room and notified of the outcome only after everyone was cleaned up. That's where I thought men belonged, but not out of some macho traditionalist mind-set. Quite the opposite. I was scared stiff that I wouldn't have the stomach for the delivery.

I had fainted at one of Jackie's early OB checkups and didn't want a repeat. I could help create a child, but would I have what it takes to help bring her into the world? Wow, I needed to man up and get it together.

Unfortunately, we lost that precious child, our first. But once things started to percolate at the delivery of our second pregnancy a few years later, my father stomach kicked in and I was totally psyched to do what I needed to do—essentially, be there for Jackie. It was the most thrilling event of my life.

By the time our fifth child was delivered, I exuded such confidence and calm that the doctor asked me if I wanted to suit up and deliver this one myself. I shot a glance at Jackie to read her thoughts on the subject. She nodded her head as if to say, "Go for it, cowboy!" The doctor talked me through it, never laying a finger on Jackie or little Isabel. I took little Izza, cut her cord, and handed her to the nurse, who handed her to Jackie. Yes, I was awesome!

At the moment when our first daughter, Olivia, arrived, we both kissed, cried, cuddled, loved, and melted all over this blessed little girl. We did the same for each of our four children after her. In each of these miraculous moments and the millions after them, we were both—as mom and dad—sending our children a vital message. By our close and intimate participation in their lives from their first days and weeks, they were each learning one of the most basic lessons about life: humanity is made up of two very different types of people. Research tells us as much.

Children quickly learn that mom is soft and pretty, smells quite nice, and has a tender, comforting voice. Dad is similar, but with notable differences. His hands are rougher, his body hairier, his face scratchier, and his voice louder and deeper. Babies find that mom and dad are different in curious and pleasant ways. Professor Henry Biller, a pioneering researcher on the parenting differences in mothers and fathers, explains how these distinctions provide early benefits:

Differences between the mother and father can be very stimulating to the infant, even those that might appear quite superficial to the adult.... The father and mother offer the child two different kinds of persons to learn about as well as providing separate but special sources of love and support. The infant also learns that different people can be expected to fulfill different needs. For example, the infant may prefer the mother when hungry or tired and the father when seeking stimulation or more active play.[2]

Because humanity is made up of only two primary types of people, we receive everyone we encounter as either male or female, which brings consequences for how we interact with others and how they interact with us. This is one of the first lessons we learn in life. Our children will continue to learn profound lessons of how male and female are different in lifelong installments as they are raised and cared for by mom and dad each day.

Understanding the differences between mother and father is like an Ivy League education for your children—one that seems nearly impossible to figure out yet is absolutely delightful and rich. We never really exhaust the depths of these sex-difference waters, but we all draw boundless riches from them in nearly every moment of life spent with others.

The first evidence of this difference in mother and father is simple and obvious. Even though infants have never heard a lecture or read any brochures on how cool moms are, they tend to be drawn early to mom over everyone else. They discern something about mom that none of the other loving and caring people in their early lives possess. Erich Fromm, in his book *The Art of Loving,* explains this connection:

The first months and years of the child are those where his closest attachment is to the mother. This attachment begins before the

moment of birth, when mother and child are still one, although
they are two. Birth changes the situation in some respects, but not
as much as it would appear. The child, while now living outside
of the womb, is still completely dependent on mother.

Fromm continues, explaining the importance of the other part of
what psychologists call the parental dyad (two parents doing their job
as parents) in the development of the child's growth, maturity, and
independence:

> But daily he becomes more independent: he learns to walk, to
> talk, to explore the world on his own; the relationship to mother
> loses some of its vital significance, and instead the relationship to
> father becomes more and more important.[3]

Fromm is correct that a baby's relationship with mom "loses some of
its vital significance" at some point in early life—usually around thirteen
to twenty-four months of age—but only in that mother is no longer the
child's *entire* world. The child begins to become aware of both himself
and his father in significant ways. Mom clearly remains vital in the child's
life, but now she does so in relation to others. Consider how monumental
this is in your child's understanding of the world. During this important
development of awareness for the child, mom becomes someone who is
not just about the new baby; she's related to others, specifically the father
as well as other siblings. The healthy child grows beyond his momma-
centric understanding of the world to rely on and draw from both parents. This is one of the child's first and earliest steps in maturity.

You might have noticed this when your toddler got nervous around
a new stranger and, instead of running to mom for comfort and security,
headed to dad for the first time—without the slightest recognition that a

profound shift had just taken place. But it was profound! Your child had matured in a healthy way.

Children desire to bond to their fathers primarily because fathers are different from mothers. They're drawn to the different kinds of experiences fathers provide. Researchers who have studied this over the past few decades note that dads tend to stimulate their infants more with excited, lively, and quickly changing facial expressions as well as more spirited vocal sounds, including words, sounds, and songs. This means that mom's voice and actions will more likely provide comfort for baby, but dad's voice and facial cues will be more exciting, unpredictable, and therefore stimulating. In other words, for the most part, dads rile babies up and mothers settle them down. Both are important.

As one professor of child psychiatry explains, fathers are unique and attractive to the child because "fathers do not mother."[4] Even in the first months of a child's life, dad tends to "engage in more physically stimulating and unpredictable play" than mother does.[5] Dr. Kyle Pruett of Yale University explains that infants seven to thirteen months of age tend to respond more positively to being held by their fathers, and while mothers tend to hold their babies for caregiving and comfort purposes, fathers are far more likely to pick up their children for play or in response to baby's requests in a greater variety of spontaneous ways. His research finds that father care tends to be more reactive than instinctual, which creates a pleasant experience of surprise and excitement for the child.[6] Pruett explains, "Fathers' typically larger size, deeper voice, coarser skin, smell, physical attributes, and habits all combine to offer a distinctively different buffet of potential attachment behaviors."[7]

Dad doesn't have the same kind of physical and emotional attachment to his baby that mom does. The father certainly has an attachment, but he has to work harder at these connections; often mom has to assist in making sure these connections get developed well.

Consider this. Do you know of dads who get jealous of the time and attention mom gives to their newborn? Of course, and more is at work here than dad's immaturity or selfishness. He's not a mom. Now, do you know of any moms who get jealous at dad's attention to their child? Perhaps no mom in the history of humanity has ever uttered the words, "You're spending way too much time with the baby, and it bothers me!" Rather, mom is likely to see dad's attention to the child as attention and care toward her. Given that father's connection to his new child is not as natural, he will often find the need to develop and improvise ways to interact with his child, like peekaboo and such. Find someone playing "ride a little horsey" with a young boy or girl and it is likely to be a man. This improvisational play from dad will tend to be more creative, more physical, and less predictable. Children come to enjoy the anticipation of the greater spontaneity, physicality, and even silliness they experience with dad.

Baby's Influence on Mom and Dad

Just as gender differences cause children to react differently to moms and dads, babies influence mothers and fathers in different ways as well. Ross Parke, a professor of psychology and a pioneering child-development theorist, finds,

> Fathers and infants, just like mothers and infants, continually
> influence each other. Fathers react to babies' signals, and
> babies, in turn, learn to use their developing communication
> skills to affect the ways their fathers treat them. These ex-
> changes teach infants an early and important lesson in social
> control: that they can influence other people through their own
> behavior.[8]

As my daughters have grown older, I have recognized how differently they interact with me in contrast to Jackie. For example, if they want something from me, they know the most likely way to get it (and no one taught them). With Jackie, they express their requests almost like demands: "Mom, I need you to take me to the mall!" With me, it's different: "Dad, you know how you said the other day that we need to spend more time together? Well, how about if we spend time while you take me to the mall to meet my friends?"

The differences between father and mother help infants, young children, and older kids all learn how their influence works and how it doesn't work. Later, we'll explore the lifelong value of this major life skill that children start to learn at a very early age.

WHAT LIES AHEAD

The difference between mom and dad benefits your children by providing a diversity of experiences, play, care, correction, encouragement, reactions, smells, feels, and sounds. Children find wonderful stimulation, challenge, and comfort in experiencing this fundamental human diversity as two distinctly different people engage in the tasks of parenting.

Psychologists, social scientists, and child-development specialists have been investigating the different ways men and women parent for nearly seventy-five years. They consistently find measurable and important differences in the ways mothers and fathers handle all kinds of important but seemingly mundane issues as they care for, play with, and simply just "be" with their children. In the following chapters, we'll explore how these differences play out in specific parenting and family activities, how the differences create a necessary and healthy balance in the development and maturity of your children, and how you can be deliberate about making the most of those differences in your parenting partnership.

———

You say that moms and dads are different, but from what you describe, I see a lot of moms doing what you say dads do, and vice versa. Are the differences really that significant?

Good question. Yes, it seems as if mothers and fathers are pretty similar in how they interact with and care for their children. But subtle and not-so-subtle differences exist. The rest of this book explores these differences in greater precision and detail regarding the different parts of parenting and child development. Suffice it to say that as researchers continue to study, they find that fathers and their fatherly ways are quite distinct from mother and her motherly ways, even if these important differences aren't always obvious to the casual observer.

———

As a father, I am interested in what you said about the ways mothers and fathers play differently with their children, even in the early weeks. Can you explain more about that?

Yes, it's fascinating stuff. Professor Alison Clarke-Stewart from the University of Chicago, one of the earliest scholars to carefully examine the distinctions of how mothers and fathers interact with infants, explains,

> Mother's role is more likely to involve physical caregiving, while the father's role involves fun and games and a link to the outside world.... Father's play was more physical, idiosyncratic, and

unpredictable and mothers' more conventional and related to materials; fathers' play involved physical tapping games, while mothers' play was verbal.[9]

From their first days, our children gain from the differences between their two parents. Our children are learning something important about themselves: they are either similar to or different from each of their parents. What that comparison reveals will have a lifelong influence on their sense of identity and their interactions with the world.

EIGHT

The Serious Business of Play

The other evening I went down to the basement to check on our two youngest. They had been down there quite some time and were much too quiet. You know the parental concern you feel at such moments.

Downstairs, I found them both sitting in chairs arranged to face each other. They were just sitting and talking to each other but in a deliberate and precise way: one asking questions and the other answering. Of course, I asked what was going on.

"We're playing *Dr. Phil*!" they answered. Tess said she was Dr. Phil and Isabel was being me. I'd been a guest on his show recently, and they were living out what they imagined the experience was like.

I found the whole scenario hilarious, but I didn't dare share that with my girls, because they were taking this very seriously. I thought, *How do kids make this stuff up?* But of course they aren't really making it up; they simply start with their understanding, however limited, of an interesting person or situation and role-play it.

For children, their work is play, and play is serious business. Play is the work that helps them become who they are meant to be. Through play, they explore and understand the world and the people who make up that world. Anthropologists teach us that play is a human universal, that children and adults in all cultures enjoy it.[1]

If you take some time to just watch your own children play (a great idea in general), you'll quickly realize that they are often replicating the world around them—or at least the way they imagine the world should be. This is a central part of becoming truly human, what pioneering child-development theorist Erik Erikson called a *sense of industry* that all healthy human beings must develop. While the word *industry* sounds a bit technical, the truth is that children develop this sense by playing all kinds of games: office, grocery store, veterinarian, or simply house. Each child takes a role and does his or her best to represent what they imagine good and interesting people do in those roles. Their busyness replicates adult business. Developing this sense of purpose is both fun and fulfilling for children.

Of course, children also play imagination games where they become actors in a more wishful world of astronauts going into space, good guys fighting bad guys from various historical periods, or kings and queens ruling mystical kingdoms. Through play, children start to learn their most serious lessons about life and who they are.

Children develop their humanity through their play. We all did.

Moms and dads also have important roles as their children play. Because of the differences in gender that we've been discussing, the dad role and mom role diverge in some key areas when it comes to playtime. This difference benefits your child. Let's start by looking at the most universal and basic view of moms and dads at play with their children: their sheer physicality.

DIFFERENT PHYSICAL INCLINATIONS, RIGHT FROM THE START

Good moms and dads are both physical with their children. However, mothers and fathers are physical in different ways, which stems from their basic nature as gendered humans.

As a mother or father, what will you do with your child in the very first moments of his or her life? Set aside any cultural or gender stereotypes you might have and think about this in the larger human experience across cultures and time. Is there a common answer? You bet there is, and it has everything to do with who we are as human beings: male or female.

A mom's overwhelming first inclination and physical activity is to take her infant close to her, comfort the newborn, and put the child to her breast for comfort and sustenance. Few if any mothers need to be taught to do this. Both mother and child receive incredible richness from this early human experience—perhaps the mom even more than the baby because everything within her needs to hold and comfort her child. Only the sheer exhaustion of delivery might keep her from it.

Dad, incredibly moved by the whole experience of birth he has just witnessed, also wants to hold and revel in the child. However, his physical response has far less to do with comforting the baby. Instead, dad wants to present his child to the world and shout, "Hey! Look what I did!"

What irony. Mom does the heavy lifting of pregnancy, labor, and delivery. Yet little within her wants the world to take notice of her work. She is focused on one concern: the new center of her world. Her husband does well to recognize this and not feel too displaced. Her only thought of others is that she wants them to be as careful with her baby as she will be—and if they aren't, only God could protect them! Mom's only thought and motivation is to focus her attention and protective nature on and glory in this child. *This is the mom-to-child orientation.*

But for dad, this new baby is many things, including a badge of honor and an amazing marker of his own significance as a man. This was true of the first man who fathered a child and every man who ever took notice of his child since. His interest is in his child and the impact this child will have on the world and vice versa.

At the birth of our oldest daughter, Olivia, I wondered for a brief second whether this new arrival would be mentioned on the local television news. To me, this was the biggest event that day in our city, if not our nation! Just as quickly, I realized that not many others felt as strongly about this amazing event as I did. What I didn't realize was that I was simply doing what fathers do—thinking about how the world would accept my child and how she would change the world. A good father will spend the next few decades caring for, providing for, protecting, and preparing this new life that he helped create for the world. *This is the dad-to-the-world and child-to-the-world orientation.*

These two orientations are generally true of mothers and fathers at every time and in every place. It's true on the sun-bathed savannas of Middle Africa and the rural rice fields of China, from the high-brow brownstones of lower Manhattan to the native mud huts of the Australian outback. In the list of human universals, this is among the most basic.

How Moms and Dads
Play Differently

As we noted previously, research indicates that infants will often respond to their fathers differently in the early weeks and months of life because babies get excited about the "roughness," unpredictability, and physicality of daddy's play.[2] One study finds that 70 percent of father-infant games are physical and action oriented while only 4 percent of mother-infant play is like this.[3] This means that baby enjoys a diversity of experiences by having both a male and a female parent, receiving physical stimulation and creativity from dad and close cuddle and care from mom. Of course, dads cuddle and snuggle too, and mothers bounce and play peekaboo with their children, but mom and dad are much more likely to do one than the other.

As children grow older, fathers will toss them in the air, wrestle with their boys and girls, and play more physically demanding and competitive games. Much of the time, fathers are more interested in playfully getting their children riled up and excited, while mothers will be more interested in comforting them and settling them down. Dads more often create controlled "crises" for sheer excitement and fun, while moms tend to be focused on averting crises.

Fathers will play the scary monster, chasing their children. And where do they run? Straight to mom, where they know they will find a safe place…and giggle uncontrollably.

Fathers are more likely to see their children as cool little people to have fun with. Mothers are more likely to see their children as little people to do things for—people who need love, comfort, and protection.

Whatever your gender-equality beliefs might be, think honestly for a moment about how you and your spouse each contribute (or wish the other contributed) to your child's play. Chances are, the differences I'm describing are generally true in your family too.

Fathers are more likely to:	_Mothers are more likely to:_
• push the limits	• mind the limits
• tickle and roughhouse	• comfort and cuddle their children
• encourage independence and confidence	• encourage dependence and security
• stress competition	• stress equity
• stress doing and accomplishing	• stress being and relationship
• encourage large-motor-skill development	• encourage fine-motor-skill development

As you ponder and discuss these differences in play, consider not just how they contrast with each other but also how they balance each other out. Your children need both of the ways mom and dad play with them.

Recognizing the value of these play differences can actually make a difference in your marriage as well, as you realize that your spouse is not trying to be contrarian or failing to understand your sensibilities. Instead, this is how God made you, along with most other mothers and fathers. When you grasp that these differences aren't personal or unique to you and your marriage and you see how they benefit your children, you can more easily negotiate a balance between your two styles, when needed.

FATHERS PUSH LIMITS AND MOTHERS MIND THEM

Go to any playground, close your eyes, and listen to the parents there. Who is saying, "Be careful!" "Not so high!" "Slow down!"? And who is saying, "Swing higher!" "Climb to the next level!" "Run faster!"?

Is it difficult to guess which statements come from dads and which come from moms? It's not gender stereotyping driving your answer. Fathers are more likely to encourage their kids to push the limits, although usually in controlled and safe ways. Mothers are interested in making sure children don't get ahead of themselves. It's not social conditioning that makes mom and dad do this. As we've seen, God wires these qualities into moms and dads. Dad helps his chicks move beyond the nest, while mom is more likely to want to keep them there, safe and sound.

I see this in myself. We have these wonderful red rock formations near our home that are world-class rock-climbing areas. Our kids like to go and scramble around the lower rocks. Something in me drives me to urge them to climb to the next handhold. Sometimes they get a little too ambitious and I have to slow them down a bit. But I want them to go as far as they can within safe limits, which usually seem to lie just beyond where Jackie would draw the line.

Dad's way keeps kids challenging themselves and succeeding. Mom's way keeps them out of the emergency room. Kids need both. Why? Because the tug of war both builds confidence through dad's "take it to the next level" encouragement and teaches reasonable caution through mom's "don't do anything you're not ready for" reminders.

As parents, we need to understand how these gender-based differences work together for our kids' healthy development. Let me explain with another example of what dads love to do with their babies.

The Upside of Throwing Babies

Last fall I visited a number of cities in China for a research and speaking trip. I spent a great deal of time just watching people interact in intimate ways: men, women, young adults, teens, children, and amazingly cute little babies. One thing I noticed was what fathers and grandfathers did with their babies. The men threw their babies gently in the air, just as they do here.

One older man in particular caught my attention. He was enjoying a Saturday morning with his granddaughter along an amazingly pictur-esque lake, throwing the little girl into the air as though she were a stuffed panda bear. It was probably the most fun she had all day, assuming that infectious giggles and laughs translate cross-culturally.

On another earlier trip I was in the Kansas City airport. The con-course there has three-quarter-height walls separating the general walk-way from gate areas. While walking to my gate, I saw an infant fly up above the wall, levitate for just a second, and then drop back down be-hind the wall. It happened again and again. Given my academic interest in such things, I surmised one of two things: either they have flying ba-bies in Kansas City, which would be pretty cool, or a parent was tossing this particular child into the air. I was betting on the second option and that it was a dad doing the tossing.

I walked around a corner where I could see the event in full through a window. Sure enough, a dad was doing the throwing, with baby com-pletely digging it—and a mom nowhere in sight.

Well, so what? What's the point?

From a child-development perspective, what was happening in the Kansas City airport and along the lake in China helps us understand how play is serious business and culturally universal. Consider being tossed in the air from the baby's perspective, who is trying to figure out this inter-esting world. These two babies—and all babies in similar situations—were learning important lessons about life. I call it the "scary world, safe world" lesson.

When babies are thrown into the air the first few times, what do they do and what are they learning?

They gasp and hold their breath, because they are literally scared breathless. You can see the fear in their eyes, as if the baby is saying, "What in the world are you doing with me? Who's the adult here?" As a dad, I have to admit, I have seen it as a look of sheer terror in my children. But it didn't stop me because the fearful look didn't last.

First lesson learned? The child is learning, in a very controlled way, that the world can be a scary place. A child isn't as likely to learn this lesson from mom because moms just aren't as likely to introduce their children to scary, challenging situations. If you're a mom and wondering why you'd ever want to introduce your child to a scary situation, your question proves the theory.

Second lesson learned? What happens to every child thrown in the air? They usually come back down. In this, the child learns the world can be a safe place in dad's hands and dad will be there to make it better. Just as quickly as that fear comes upon them as they are tossed into the air, they come safely down into the comforting hands of dad. Within the space of a moment, they are experiencing two very raw and deeply instructive emotions. At one point their whole being screams out, "Holy cannoli, I don't like this!" Then just as quickly, as the babies land back in the strong and reassuring grasp of their dads, they experience, "Oh good, the world is now safe." Then another feeling comes upon them: "Let's do it again!"

If you doubt all this, think about yourself. The same dynamic has made those in the roller-coaster business very rich. Most of us love this controlled rush of possible danger and then safety again.

With babies, this process is more than just fun. The child learns that scary things will come in life but she'll be okay and she can count on dad to take care of her. This builds both confidence and comfort. Moms build comfort in their children in other ways, like holding them close.

This is also essential, because if children are able to operate from a position of security and acceptance, they won't have difficulty doing anything else in life. The security that mom provides is the launching pad for our children, and it should follow them all of their lives. But the different kind of security that dad provides through helping children successfully face challenges and fear is important as well. Both parents provide security, but dad's way is more likely to build confidence as kids learn about taking risks and recovering safely from them.

A counselor friend told me a story that illustrates this truth. One of his adult clients was struggling with trust issues. See if you can figure out why. The client told of playing with his father one day. Dad would have the boy jump off the porch steps and into his arms. With each jump, dad would take a step back, requiring the boy to jump farther and harder, taking a greater risk. This young boy was learning that he could take chances and succeed in hitting the mark: his dad's arms. When dad was quite some ways from the porch, he encouraged the boy to give it all he had and jump. While the boy was in midair, the father backed up a few steps, leaving his son to land right on his face on the concrete walkway. The boy's life and conception of the world changed dramatically as he hit the ground. He glared up at his father with a look that screamed, "Why did you do that? I was depending on you!" The dad looked sternly at the boy and said, "Just a little lesson, son! Never, ever trust anyone!"

Sadly, that's exactly what the boy grew up to do. He couldn't even trust his father, someone he should always be able to trust. As a result, he couldn't trust himself either. He had no confidence. This lousy father demonstrates for us, in the extreme negative, the value of having a good father who can be counted on.

Fathers who provide safe chance-taking opportunities provide something essential for healthy children: confidence. And with confidence, an essential type of security.

ROUGHHOUSING AND SELF-CONTROL

Just as children learn lessons in midair, more things happen down on the floor with dad and child. And it includes more than making a lot of noise and potentially breaking stuff. Through roughhousing with dads, children learn an essential life lesson that will serve them well: self-control.

Fathering expert John Snarey explains that older children who roughhouse with their fathers learn by experience to control their own aggression and anger. While wrestling with my own children, I've been bitten, kicked, and jumped on. It is just what excited kids do. I remember one time when Schaeffer was younger and we were wrestling on the floor. He was small, and I was being gentle with him. I was on all fours, and he was on my back with his arms around my neck. I reared up like a horse, and he loved it. I then felt this sharp bite to my shoulder. It startled me, and it hurt pretty good. I remember reacting starkly because I didn't expect him to be a biter quite yet. I felt bad for yelling at him. Yet Schaeffer learned quickly that biting dad isn't a good idea.

So it is with most dads and their kids. Children learn self-control by being told when "enough is enough" and when and how to "shut it down."[4] Children—particularly boys—who don't have these teachable moments with dad tend to be too rough and physically hurt others (usually unintentionally) as they grow. Their internal self-control mechanism hasn't been properly calibrated.

Watch boys at a birthday party who seem to have no appreciation for limits in noise or in play. Perhaps even you have a boy who hasn't gained this important self-control lesson from his dad. He jumps into the ball pit with everything he has and without the slightest thought for who he is jumping on. Both moms and dads teach this kind of self-control, but dads teach it more dramatically because the lesson is usually learned in the process of play. Men have performed this important task for millenniums, and mothers have recognized and appreciated the value of it.

The development of self-control leads to the development of two other important qualities that both mother and father develop in children: competition and equity.

COMPETITION AND EQUITY

Notice how dads and moms play games with children. Which parent is more likely to be interested in who's winning or what strategy will secure a victory? Who's looking to make sure everyone is having fun and being fair? Of course, there's not a perfect divide in these areas, yet fathers are often more interested in the outcome of the game, while mothers are more interested in how all are faring in the process. Both are important.

My daughter's basketball coach wanted the team to play the parents in a practice game. It turned out to be all dads. Throw a ball to a man, and competitiveness kicks in, even when playing his twelve-year-old daughter. It wasn't too ugly, but it was palpable. Even I felt it, and I'm not a team sports guy at all. Sophie caught my eye during the game and gave me a look that clearly said, "Dad, chill! We're twelve-year-old girls!" The coach knew what he was doing. He wanted the girls to face some stiff but measured competition and in the process build the girls' confidence.

Moms on the court in such a game would be more likely to make sure the girls got the ball enough and could get some easier steals than the dads allowed them to have. In fact, the coach's wife, who also coached the team and is a very competitive woman, checked any of the dads she covered pretty aggressively to make sure they brought it down a notch for fairness. She was the equalizer.

Again, both ways are correct. Mom's way gives hope and fairness. Dad's way presses the children to push themselves. Children need to learn both in games and in life. How annoying is it to have someone who constantly makes sure all are treated fairly in a game, as if that's the only thing that counts? But even worse is someone who always has to win at any cost. Balance is key.

Doing Versus Relating

Closely related to competition and equity is the difference and balance between *doing* and *relating*. In their play with parents, children are more likely to learn from dad the importance of seeing a task through, while mom will teach the importance of making sure people are cared and provided for. Why? For men, success is measured by whether a goal is accomplished and how it gets accomplished. For women, success is more about how people connected and developed in the process. This seems like an odd contrast, but see if you recognize it in your own family interactions.

Picture a family making cupcakes. For mom, the activity would be more about the process. She will be more willing to let the kids do the measuring, mixing, and pouring, not caring if things get a little off track or if the process takes three times as long to complete. The kids are having a good time and having an important experience. She relishes the experience for herself and her children. While not opposed to any of this, dad has the end result in mind. He has a mission to accomplish, even if that mission is only cupcakes. His gut wants to show his kids how to get the task done. Only when the cupcakes are baked, frosted, and ready to eat is the mission accomplished for dad.

Here's what's cool: kids need both. Relationships are much more important than accomplishing things. But in the work world all of us eventually enter, the boss will want results and children need to learn how to deliver them.

LARGE- AND FINE-MOTOR SKILLS

The gender-based differences in how parents play even help children develop the two kinds of motor skills their bodies need to function.

Father play is more likely to stimulate large-motor-skill growth: sitting up, tumbling, balancing, rolling, throwing, jumping, catching, or running. Mother play encourages fine-motor-skill growth: eating, dressing, doing finger play, coloring, cutting, or tying. In general, dads teach kids to use their bodies more while moms teach kids to use their hands more. Both are important and needed because they are both parts of being physically coordinated and capable people. One can't be ignored for the sake of the other.

Think about an invitation from an adult for a child to go play tag or climb on the jungle gym. Or another invitation to sit at the kitchen table to color and paint or to cut out and glue papers. Which are you and your spouse more likely to welcome the child to do? What's good for the child? Both, right? Because they need a balance, and that's what you and your spouse provide.

THE WONDERFUL WORLD OF PLAY

We've seen how both mom and dad help their children explore the fullness of their serious world of play. Without realizing it, parents often do this in very different ways according to their own sex distinction. But children benefit deeply from this developmental process in countless ways.

Mothers and fathers hold their children differently in relation to the larger world. Moms provide protection and dads encourage opportunity. Good mothers help their children become aware of limits, and good fathers help their children challenge limits safely. Through roughhousing and physical play, dads teach boys and girls not only how to demonstrate their energy, physical strength, and coordination but also how to control and use those in productive and safe ways. Moms teach fairness in play and how to watch out for and take consideration for others. This is vital for human beings. Dads, while not primarily concerned with this, teach it as well by showing children how to seek to win while being fair and considerate of others. And lastly, fathers help develop their children's large motor skills by engaging in play that makes use of the whole body. Mothers help children develop their fine motor skills by encouraging activities that require use of the hands and more precise control.

So play with your children, and realize that your spouse has a different way of playing. The difference is valuable to your kids' sense of risk and safety as well as to their sense of competition and equity, all contributing to their increased sense of self-control, confidence, and security. And as you play with your children, see if you can increasingly notice what they are learning and gaining in the process and how both you and your spouse contribute to that.

———

Q You say that boys learn confidence from their fathers. Do girls learn confidence from their fathers or mothers?

A Actually both boys and girls learn confidence from both mother and father, in different ways. But confidence is more deeply impacted by dad for both boys and girls. Whenever I meet a strong, intelligent, and confident young woman in my travels, I ask her to tell me about growing up in her family. It's very rare if these women don't talk about a caring father who invested a great deal in them.

A girl is created to desire the appreciation and attention of a man. When she gets good, healthy, and affirming attention from her father, she receives an almost daily message that she matters in a zillion different ways. This makes her attractively secure and confident.

———

You talked about the play of very young children. Our toddler-age son has an older sister, and sometimes he plays dress up with her and ends up in a dress. Do we need to be concerned about this?

The easy answer to this question is there's not really healthy or unhealthy sex-specific play for very young toddlers. While their sense of play has definitely kicked in by the early toddler years, their sense of gender self-awareness has not.

Toddlers are just entering a deeper phase of self-discovery through play, but they haven't yet learned or sensed that some types of play are more interesting to boys and others more intriguing for girls. This lack of knowledge is good and natural at this age.

When our son Schaeffer was a toddler, he was the only boy in a home with two sisters. Often, with his sisters at playtime, Schaeffer was as interested in the dresses in the playclothes basket as he was in the boy stuff. While this concerned me a little bit, it shouldn't have. He was a two-year-old boy with two sisters. He was being a part of the crowd he lived in, joining in on the game, and the game was usually what the girls were doing. He wasn't acting contrary to his sex. His psychological awareness of his maleness hadn't really started in full yet. Sure, he knew he was a boy, but he'd never been a boy before, so he was a little weak on the dos and don'ts of boyhood. He would start getting this as he grew because he would observe older boys and we'd help him along the way. But it's not like the concrete sets for good in the first twenty minutes. It happens over the next two or three years.

Systematic studies show that boys and girls will start to engage in more gender-preferred play at around age three:

> Boys are said to be more interested in cars, trucks, and airplanes, as well as guns and swordlike objects, and to like making noises that are appropriate to these toys: motor sounds, siren noises, shouts of bang-bang. Boys are also said to be more interested in building blocks and mechanical toys, including robots. Infants and toddlers of both sexes like teddy bears and other stuffed animals, but girls are thought to be more interested in dolls, and many parents notice that even at the age of 2, girls especially like to dress up in party clothes and adorn themselves with jewelry and hair ribbons.[5]

As boys and girls gradually diverge into distinct play preferences, how do parents determine what's healthy and what's not? As your little one goes through this slow phase of gender self-discovery, he or she will start to identify more with boy or girl things. Parents can regularly and subtly demonstrate what boy play is and what girl play is by demonstrating and inviting as needed. The same-gender parent can present the world of men or women as a secret society that the child is just gaining access to. This is huge for kids—to be invited and encouraged into something special.

As children grow past the toddler years, the importance of teaching children sex differentiation is important. It's also humanly universal. All cultures have recognized that their children need some guidance in navigating these differences.

———

Is there a connection between violence among boys and the increases we've been seeing in fatherlessness?

A profound and direct connection! You see, boys who wrestle and rough-house physically with their fathers learn both self-control and physical confidence. Ever seen an excited and playful boy jump on or kick his father in the crotch? The boy will quickly learn about boundaries and what he shouldn't do. Better to learn this from dad than from another boy on the playground.

Perhaps more important, in the physicality of playing with dad, the boy is also being affirmed; even though he might not ever pin his father while wrestling, he'll come closer and closer as he gets older and bigger. A good father will affirm his son's strength and skill through this process.

Boys who don't grow up getting this affirmation from their fathers will have a great drive to prove to the world what their fathers never affirmed in them—that they are people to be respected. They will typi-cally end up demanding this respect from the community in unhealthy ways.

Forty years ago, such boys would show forth their masculinity—seeking to prove what they deeply doubt—through womanizing and fast, loud cars. Today, they show this through womanizing and violence. A young gangbanger with a gun is trying desperately to scream to the world, "I am someone to reckon with and you *will* respect me!" Unfortunately, they get anything but respect.

NINE

How Moms and Dads Together Influence Language Development

For a few years, at the time our twins were learning to talk, we lived in the deepest end of the Deep South. They had a few little playmates who spoke with amazingly thick Southern accents—sorghum molasses thick. You'd have thought they talked that way to lampoon Southern folks, as if they were characters in a *Saturday Night Live* skit. But that's just how they talked.

Jackie and I were a bit concerned that our kids might start speaking this way also, simply because we lived in this part of the country. But guess what? They ended up speaking just like mom, dad, older sister, and extended family.

Children learn speech from those around them, day in and day out. My brother and his wife adopted an amazing little boy from Mexico.

One of our kids asked why Joshua didn't have an accent. The answer is that we develop our language from home, not from our heritage or larger environment. Our kids learn to talk through the continual verbal stimulation of their parents. As child-development expert Henry Biller explains, "Young children who are exposed to very little verbal attention from other family members are more likely to develop language difficulties than those who are the recipients of at least a moderate amount of communication."[1]

Have you ever thought about how important language is in child development? Consider that it's the first sophisticated and really human thing your child will learn and do. And think of what a big deal language is. It's certainly a big deal for those of us with a Christian view of reality. Before anything else, there was a community of divine persons: Father, Son, and Holy Spirit. This community of Three accomplished the work of creating by…snapping their fingers? clapping? No, They accomplished Their creative work by speaking! *God said…and it was.*

God spoke and it was so, for every part of the created universe.

Communication isn't a created thing. As a quality of God, it didn't have a beginning. Think about the first human qualities we develop. It's not the need for or ability to sleep, eat, or move around. Animals instinctually do each of these, so they're not uniquely human. But we need love, while animals don't. We need to communicate with words. These make us human because they are two qualities that God gives to and shares with us. Therefore, communication is a divine quality, and because we are image bearers of God, it's also a human quality. Keep that in mind as you think about your child's language development. As your child begins to speak, yes, be blown away that he can say "dada" and "mama." But also remember that your child is starting to blossom as a unique God-imager in the world.

Words and More: Verbal Communication

Because mom and dad are different types of parents, our children learn different but essential things from both.

Pediatricians and child-development scholars have known for decades that infants in their earliest weeks learn to distinguish the voices of mom and dad. As this takes place, they slowly begin to respond differently to mom or dad. They couldn't do this if discernible differences didn't exist between the two.

As we noted before, dads will tend to use a louder and more declarative voice, while moms use a softer and more reassuring voice. Watch mothers. They tend to talk to an infant in ways that encourage and develop closeness, tenderness, and security. Fathers talk to their infants in ways more likely to stimulate reaction and excitement from them. Again, moms are more likely to get baby settled down, while fathers want to get baby worked up. Your child is learning, from a very early age, that different voices and tones are indeed different, getting different reactions and responses.

Research explains that fathers are more likely than mothers to be directive, speaking in a staccato rhythm. But they also tend to use longer explanations with their children. Mothers are more predictable and repetitive as well as singsong in their communication with the child.[2] As children grow, fathers are more likely to ask questions and dig for answers. This develops more of a sense of participation as well as challenge for the child. Mothers ask questions more along the lines of, "Did you find your sock?" or, "Would you like to go outside and swing?" or, "Would some juice be nice?" This certainly isn't because moms are simpler and dads more sophisticated. Instead, moms are more focused on meeting the needs of children and more attuned to connecting, while fathers are more interested in doing things and getting reactions from their children. Without even thinking about it, dads will often ask basic but compound questions, requiring children to consider more than one idea at a time. A dad, for example, might say, "What do you want to do after lunch? Take Sam for a walk by the lake, or go play in the leaves in the backyard?" The child can make the choice based on a number of considerations or decide if she wants to offer a third alternative. Mom's and dad's ways of communicating are both very loving and caring but different, as sure as dad's hands and cheeks have a very different feel than mom's.

Fathers are also more likely to make reference to past events, applying them to the present, than are mothers. Often a dad isn't aware that such concepts might be beyond his child's stage of development. However, this serves to push and challenge the child. Sometimes a dad does realize a concept is too advanced for his child, and it reminds him his child is indeed a child. In any event, the child is learning and being encouraged to expand his ability to consider larger concepts like his place in the relations of past, present, and future.

Perhaps the biggest and most consequential difference between the ways moms and dads communicate is their use of words. Mothers are more likely to simplify their words and speak on the child's level. Most men aren't as inclined to modify their language for children, simply because they're less likely to be aware they need to. As Eleanor Maccoby, a groundbreaking scholar on gender difference and child development from Stanford, explains, "The mother's mean length of utterance is more closely related to that of the child she is addressing than is the father's, and...fathers used more unfamiliar, difficult, or specialized words" with their children.[3]

How does this benefit your child? Mom's way facilitates immediate communication between child and parent. This is good in that it provides a secure and close connection between mother and child. Your child loves this! Dad's way is more likely to instigate a vocabulary lesson. While this can be a wee bit frustrating for child and father, it does tend to stretch and challenge a young mind. Your child benefits richly from this stretching.

I remember realizing this when our children were young. I researched these gender differences during the day at work and then unwittingly observed them at home in the evenings. One of the kids would do something naughty, and Jackie would say, "Tess, no-no!" Or maybe just, "Tess!" with the look that only moms can give. Tess knew exactly what mom meant. If a similar behavior happened with me, I would say, "Tess, listen. That behavior is entirely inappropriate, and you are getting much too old to act like that anymore!" I actually remember saying something like this to Tess years ago, and she responded back, "Daddy, what means 'inappropriate'?" I received her indirect message that kids aren't adults and you have to speak to them as kids.

When our kids got older, I started explaining what I meant, and together we expanded their vocabularies with useful new words. I recognized that this happened often with the kids and me when we interacted. It's not that I have a more sophisticated vocabulary than Jackie by any means but simply that she had a better grasp of who she was talking to. Note if this is true in your home. Children with fathers in the home tend to have more advanced vocabulary development than kids who live apart from their fathers.[4] Increased vocabulary development provides the foundation for and feeds nearly every future educational pursuit. It also gives your child greater confidence to speak up in class and to other adults they meet. Vocabulary is the basic building block of learning.

Also, mom is likely to better understand baby's unique way of asking for something than dad can. The baby will declare very emphatically, "Mo hashi mek, mo hashi mek!" and slam the cup down. Mom knows exactly what's needed. She explains to dad, "He wants more chocolate milk!" and dad wonders how she ever discerned that. When mom isn't around, as dad and child try to make these connections on their own, both baby and daddy learn how real understanding can be achieved. The child learns when dad finally figures it out and says, "Oh, I get it. You want more chocolate milk." Eventually, the child will start saying words more like dad says them because that's how daddy understands it; mom and baby never have such an interaction because mom more intuitively gets what's being said.

Mom's communication provides predictability and security of connection. Dad's initiates more of a classroom experience. So which way of communicating with our kids is best—mom's or dad's? The answer is that both are right.

SPEAKING WITHOUT WORDS: NONVERBAL COMMUNICATION

Nonverbal communication is another vital aspect of teaching our children to live well in the world. Learning nonverbal communication is essential because our most important communication takes place through facial expressions, bodily adjustments, a certain but subtle tilt of the head, and unarticulated hums and grunts. Statements like, "I really like that hat!" or, "I'm so glad you stopped by!" can take on two very opposite meanings depending merely on facial expression. We are handicapped as communicators if we don't learn to read these cues. So this is an essential part of what our children must learn as growing communicators.

Both moms and dads communicate clear messages of approval, encouragement, disapproval, and excitement in the most subtle of ways. Amazingly, our children learn these quickly, without either parent or child really being aware of it.

Dad can furrow his brow. Mom can raise an eyebrow. Dad can wink. Mom can smile. Children know what each of these subtle messages means and where they stand with each one. As parents, we also learn how to give looks to our children that might appear corrective, but our children know because of very slight adjustments, we actually mean, "Okay, go ahead…this time!" The difference and comfort in these cues is slight but significant.

A girl growing up day after day with her father learns over the years how to have a complete conversation with dad at the breakfast table as he sits behind his paper giving nothing but grunts and hums in response to what she says and asks. She knows by reading nonverbal cues with amazing insight whether to ask mom or dad about scoring some extra money to catch a movie with friends.

Likewise, a boy learns from his mom how to communicate with a woman—when to push a little harder and when he absolutely should not. He learns when to use a particular tone or not. He learns over time what exactly will push her "yes" or her "back it down, mister!" buttons. He also learns how to comfort mom when she gets hurt. A boy who is both well mothered and well fathered will be more sensitive to women as he grows. He learns much of this by just reading their nonverbal cues and reactions to others.

The Ultimate Language School

Girls learn from fathers how to communicate and negotiate confidently with men. Boys learn how to communicate and deal graciously and respectfully with women when they see a father demonstrate it and a mother demand it through healthy communication and proper expectations.

Our children pick up so much more than we imagine by simply communicating with mom and dad in the daily warp and woof of life.

These lessons are taught and learned in a zillion different ways and situations even when both parent and child are unaware they're participating in a language lesson.

—

You talked about children gaining a great vocabulary from their fathers. I agree, but some of the words my husband indirectly teaches our children are not the kinds of words any child should be learning. What should I do when these vocabulary lessons aren't desirable and beneficial?

I'm amazed how quickly young children pick up and repeat words their parents use—even the rarest curse word from their lips. This is why parenting carries with it a large responsibility.

I remember helping a man work on his car when I was a teenager. His toddler son was milling about as we worked, and the man and I talked the whole time about the work we were doing and other guy stuff. The man stripped a bolt he was working on, busted his knuckles, and then ceremoniously damned that very bolt to the fiery pit. Of all the words we'd been uttering, his son picked up on that one phrase. He just kept repeating it over and over again, and his father was too angry and preoccupied to notice. I tried not to laugh, and I gave the boy a lesson in nonverbal communication by catching his gaze with my intent look and shaking my head back and forth firmly in a clear no-no fashion. He stopped repeating the words—at least for the time being.

Those occasions where kids encounter vulgar terms or swear words provide the opportunity to teach that such words aren't acceptable. Of course, it's better if kids aren't introduced to such words at all, especially by their own parents. But inevitably your child will hear new and intriguing words when you're out shopping or playing at the park. When our children are young, they don't distinguish between acceptable and unacceptable, but as they grow, they'll recognize inappropriate words and invariably look to mom or dad for their reaction. Parents should communicate either through words or clear disapproving looks that such words are distasteful or off-limits.

It's important to talk together as parents about what words and attitudes in our communication are healthy—or not—for our children. And we must be open to the advice and thoughts of our spouses, given their unique perspective on life and children. Mom should be able to remind dad that "your golf words" are not appropriate at home, and dad might need to remind mom that, "Yes indeed, the kids picked up on the snarky comment you made about Mrs. Wade's sweater with the big deer head embroidered on the front."

We are always teaching our kids with our speech. Both parents should pay attention, praising each other when they do it well and providing gentle correction when they don't! It's what parents do.

TEN

Balancing Grace
and Discipline

When I was a boy and even through my adulthood, my father was pretty tough on me. He couldn't seem to pass up an opportunity to turn nearly every experience into a teachable moment—even when I was a forty-something professional man with a wife and five children.

When I was a teenager and still living at home, each day brought my dad numerous opportunities to make me a better person. I had a good friend, Michael, whose father gave him little attention. While I felt I lived on a pretty short leash, Michael had no leash at all. He was drawn to my father in those teen years. Although I would have given just about anything to get out from under my father's thumb, I wouldn't have traded his high-control approach for the "freedom" that Michael had.

We show our children love when we correct and discipline them, even when we do so imperfectly. Kids might not place discipline in the top ten list of things they appreciate about their parents, but most realize, deep down, that correction and parameters are an expression of love. They provide security.

Dr. James Dobson illustrated this truth in a story about what happened at a particular school yard many years ago. This newly built school was situated near a busy four-lane highway, and the school's playground sat on the side of the school that paralleled the highway. Given the rush and roar of traffic, the children all huddled closely to the playground equipment near the side of the school building. Few of them ran and played freely in the large field between the monkey bars and the highway. When an eight-foot fence was finally erected around the property, bordering the road, something interesting happened to the play patterns of the kids. They started using the whole area of the playground, places they never ventured pre-fence, even playing right up against the fence within feet of the roadway.

Why the dramatic shift in play habits? With no protective boundaries, the children felt vulnerable. The boundary of the fence created security and a carefree feeling for the kids. Ironically, the fence set them free.

Perhaps this story seems overly simple or obvious. But the concept holds true regarding the discipline and correction of our children. Most parents don't struggle with whether to provide a lot of discipline or no discipline. We struggle to find the proper balance and mix of discipline needed to provide our children with this essential form of love and direction.

The gender-distinct ways that moms and dads tend to approach discipline is critical in developing a healthy balance for our children and our homes. So let's explore the question: how do moms and dads mete out correction and discipline differently, and how do these differences benefit our children?

OPPOSITE BUT ESSENTIAL

In many ways, both mother and father reflect the two sides of God as He responds to our disobedience. He is both firm and judging but also gracious and forgiving. These responses seem contradictory, but they are essential to each other.

Think about the messages of John the Baptist and Jesus. Which would you rather sit and listen to for an afternoon? John directly told you where you stood and expected you to do something about it. Jesus, however, was softer and more helpful in the sense of offering His hearers insight, wisdom, hope, and direction in living in the kingdom of God. Yet Jesus said there was no greater man than John the Baptist. Parents can do things very differently and both be right.

Harvard educational psychologist Carol Gilligan is on the more radical end of the feminist movement. But her earliest research involved male and female differences. In her celebrated book *In a Different Voice,* she tells us that fathers stress justice, fairness, and duty (based on rules), while mothers are more likely to stress sympathy, grace, care, and help (based on relationships).[1]

A recent event made me realize how accurate this description of moms and dads is. Jackie called to ask if Sophie had left her science folder in my car when I dropped her and the other kids off at school that morning. Sophie needed it for school and wasn't sure where it was. I told Jackie that the kids left nothing in the backseat, so she said she'd look for it at home and take it up to Sophie. Because the school is a pretty good haul from our house, this meant at least an hour of Jackie's time. I was inclined to say, "If Sophie needed her notebook so badly, she should have kept track of where it was. Doing without her notebook today might be a good reminder of that." In other words, let her learn by facing the hard, cold facts of reality. But I didn't. Good thing.

Jackie said she didn't want to spend the time hunting down the notebook and driving it to the school but she would because she didn't want Sophie worrying about it all day. As Jackie started to look around the house, Sophie called and said she found her notebook buried in her locker.

It struck me how Jackie and I responded so differently to the situation. Both reactions were based on what would be best for Sophie. Jackie's intention was to relieve her of anxiety. Mine was to give her reason to think more carefully about how she manages her school supplies. My way has its time, but I think Jackie made the right call, given Sophie's personality and nature.

A leading sociologist on mother-father parenting differences, David Popenoe from Rutgers has been a good friend and teacher to me for more than a decade. He explains,

> The disciplinary approach of fathers tends to be "firm" while that of mothers tends to be "responsive." Mothers' discipline varies more from time to time, involves more bargaining and is adjusted to the child's mood and context. It is seemingly based on a more intuitive understanding of the child's needs and emotions of the moment. Fathers, without the "special understanding" of mothers, necessarily rely on rules and principles. Based on this distinction, of course, mothers are often accused of being too soft, while fathers are accused of being too arbitrary and rigid.[2]

AIMING FOR BALANCE

Our children need the two different ways mothers and fathers provide correction. Fathers tend to enforce rules sternly and objectively, looking at the situation. Mothers tend to enforce rules relative to the state of the child, with grace and sympathy. Dad's concern about the rules teaches children the objectivity and consequences of right and wrong. Mom's approach affirms the importance of feelings and relationships and undergirds a sense of hopefulness in the child.

Which one is best? As you might guess, living under both is necessary because of the way the world works and because of the nature of the human heart. Let me explain.

Imagine trying to explain to a police officer that you are speeding because you're late to pick up your child at school and that you wouldn't be speeding under other circumstances. Most likely, that ticket has your name on it and your story will do nothing to move this law enforcement officer. Now imagine trying to explain that you are speeding to get to the hospital because your husband cut off three of his fingers with a power saw. Imagine him saying, "Well, I'll get you on your way just as soon I finish writing this ticket!" The point is, there's a time for hard-core rule following and a time for understanding. If our children get doses of just one or the other in their developing years, something unhealthy takes place.

When parents give children nothing but grace and consistently justify disobedience based on the circumstances, their children will likely grow up to have problems with folks and institutions that lean "black and white," like the law, the IRS, the DMV, college professors, and officials at athletic competitions. Yet when parents give kids nothing but stern and unforgiving enforcement of rules and regulations, their children become hopeless, depressed, insecure, and untrusting. Often, as soon as they are out from under the parental thumb, these kids go absolutely nuts in rebellion.

Kids need a healthy balance of both styles of parental correction and discipline. They must learn that life will present times when absolute obedience is mandatory and correct. April 15 is one example. However, kids must also learn that sometimes love and care mean some slack in the rope. Moms and dads need to work in tandem to balance each other in the application of discipline and correction.

This balance reminds me of the spiritual issues of truth and grace that often seem to be in tension. Should faithful Christians advocate the absoluteness of truth or the forgiveness of grace? While we struggle with how, most of us know that these two realities should always balance each other. Focusing on one to the exclusion of the other leads to an unhealthy view of God.

Many times, there's no absolute right answer for whether mom and dad's discipline decisions should fall on the side of grace or on the side of firmness. Where you land depends on the character of each of you as parents. Do you tend more toward bending the rules or keeping them rigid? Do both of you tend toward the same extreme, or does only one of you lean toward one end of the discipline spectrum?

My mom and dad were very different. However, my mother wasn't strong enough to exert any influence to balance out my father. Ideally, as a mom and dad you will both see the benefits of each way of disciplining your children and will work together to agree on which response is called for in a particular circumstance.

Of course, your child's temperament also matters. Is your child naturally hard on himself, often feeling that his best isn't good enough? Then you may want to land on the side of grace with discipline and correction, because he needs to learn to go easier on himself. He needs to realize that things will be fine if he doesn't knock every ball out of the park. On the other hand, do you have a child who is a genius at cutting the corners in her favor? She could use a bit more black and white, helping her realize that everyone has expectations to live up to. Where you land with each child might change from time to time and from age to age. Both mom and dad should be mindful of these temperaments and changes in their children and adjust accordingly.

Most often, when mom and dad work together and understand the propensity of each toward one of the poles of hard and soft, law and grace, they can strike a balance that responds effectively to their child's unique blend.

When it comes to discipline, your children will benefit immeasurably from two parents who appreciate their shared wisdom and differing tendencies.

I see the differences you've described in my own family. It has caused problems for my husband and me. He says that my grace toward our children's behavior is more sentimental, while his firmer discipline is more "real world," as he calls it. How can we both see the benefit of each approach?

I think many parents struggle with this issue. Most of us naturally see our way as the right way. Every husband and wife must realize that both the mom way of parenting and the dad way of parenting are God-given gifts. By working together, you can arrive at the healthy and proper balance your children need. This is how God wired the parenting partnership.

So "real world" fathers need to understand this critical balance, and so do "let's give them a break" mothers. The goal is to temper each other. Sometimes couples who struggle with striking a balance can consult other family members or friends who have found their way to the middle ground. However, you need to seek this counsel from parents whom both of you trust and respect. Otherwise you'll see the advice as coming from someone who is naturally prejudiced against either firmness or grace.

———

I recognize what you're saying about moms and dads in other couples we know. But my spouse and I tend to reflect the qualities you've attributed to moms. How can we seek balance when both of us approach discipline the same way?

You might find it curious to hear me answer that you probably don't have to be so mindful of this. Did I just refute everything we just discussed? Not at all!

If your child tends to be more demanding of himself, then you don't have to be as aware of this distinction in approaches; your child is already oriented toward meeting the bar. In fact, he needs help letting himself fail from time to time and being able to live with that.

If your child isn't demanding of himself, you and your spouse need to carefully discuss what expectations and rules your child might need as well as how firmly you should enforce the rules. If neither of you are oriented to be hard liners, you'll need to be more deliberate about building up this part of your child's developmental process. While these tendencies are distinct along gender lines, it's not as important that dad is "black and white" and mom is more compassionate. Rather, it's important that each perspective is present to some degree and can balance the other out.

In Jackie's family, her father was that rare man who was the more gracious and forgiving one, while her mom was more of a warden—but she served that role with tremendous grace. In fact, Jackie's mom still displays that quality wonderfully with her grandkids, and they all love her endlessly for it.

ELEVEN

Preparation Versus Protection: Why Both Dad and Mom Are Right

When my brother Todd and I were young, I remember our dad teaching us how to fight. Not each other—we didn't need any help there. He wanted us to know how to protect ourselves in the scrappy neighborhood where we lived.

This education took two forms. The first involved proper lessons in boxing. He bought us each a pair of red lace-up boxing gloves and took us out to the back patio to run through some basics: how to hold up our dukes so our faces were guarded, how to punch strategically, and how to block punches coming at us.

Then he had us go at it! We were like two young spinning windmills, wildly pitching our blades at each other, creating a lot of wind, but doing little damage to each other. I remember being disappointed. We wanted to knock each other out, not from anger or hatred, but simply because it looked cool when Muhammad Ali and George Foreman did it on television.

I remember that those lessons wore my arms out—not so much from punching but from holding my arms up in a boxing stance for so long. I also remember how it felt to have real boxing gloves strapped on my wrists—just like a real boxer! This was one of the first "real man" things I ever did. I also remember how frustrated I got because, no matter how hard I punched Todd, nothing seemed to faze him because of the gloves. It was like whacking someone with two big marshmallows. Punching to no effect is no fun.

The other way our dad taught us to fight was more school yard or guerrilla style. His technique consisted of one move, which seemed a little strange to me. He wanted to send us out into the mean streets of our neighborhood, with its resident bullies and bruisers, equipped to defend ourselves with just one move? It seemed we'd need more than that, but one was all we got.

Here was the secret weapon. First, the bully or attacker had to approach you from the front for the move to work. So essentially you had to secure your assailant's cooperation with the plan in order to defeat him. This also struck me as curious. Anyway, as your attacker is coming at you, you reach out quickly with both hands and grab his biceps right above the elbows and hang on. Once attached to the thug this way, you fall backward to the ground, landing on your back, pulling your assailant with you. As you both fall, you raise one of your legs—either one will do—and drive it into his gut. As your back hits the ground, you use your arms and extended leg to pull the attacker-turned-victim over yourself as if you are two circus tumblers; he flies into the air and then over your head and to the ground. Dad had Todd and me practice on each other a number of times, and after a few rough starts it worked like a charm. Your victim might not be hurt when he hits the ground, but he's certainly surprised that you got the first shot in so quickly.

I guess this factor was what made the move so effective in my dad's mind. He never explained to us what came next, and we never asked. But now I presume you would use that element of surprise to move yourself to safety. While none of this made sense to me at the time, I can now see the wisdom, given the paper-thin veneer of an adolescent bully's frail machismo. The hurled bruiser, lying on the ground, would wonder what other tricks you might have up your sleeve and decide just to give you a wide berth in the weeks and months to come. This would also effectively protect you from the other bullies. Of course, no self-respecting bully would tell his thug pals what happened, but he would spread the word that you weren't worth bothering with.

I'm sure our mom said to Dad, "Bill, do you really have to teach the boys to be so rough, encouraging them to hurt others? Why don't we teach them to settle problems with their words?" You see, the soundtrack of my childhood home came from the constant spinning of my mom's LPs that featured songs like Cat Stevens's "Peace Train" and "Moonshadow." We ingested them like secondhand smoke because she played those records relentlessly during the day while Dad was at work. She tried to turn us into little brainwashed peaceniks, but it never really took. So she wasn't keen on Dad's militaristic training sessions.

How Moms and Dads View Danger

This story from my childhood illustrates the different perspectives mothers and fathers hold regarding their children and the imminent dangers of the world. Once we're aware of this difference, it's interesting to observe it in our families and those around us.

Consider the statements below. Which are dads more likely to say to their children? Which are moms more likely to say?

- "Are you going to let that kid talk to you like that?"
- "That hill looks awfully steep. You'd better stand over here by me!"
- "That hill looks awfully steep. Let me show you how much fun you can have sliding down it on a flattened cardboard box!"
- "You're going out without your coat?"
- "Let's walk over here. There might be snakes in those woods."
- "Let me show you how to tell if a snake is nonpoisonous and then how to catch it safely."
- "I wonder if you could jump down from that limb."
- "Let me teach you how to safely cross a busy street like this."
- "I think it's best if you don't go near that busy street."

Mothers are far more likely to see the dangers of the world as something to protect their children from. A mom will build a protective wall between her child and any possible threat, real or imagined. Her most basic orientation from the beginning of her mothering process is protective. She receives, takes in, and cares for that which she is given.

Fathers are much more likely to see the dangers of the world as something to prepare their children for. Dads want to take their children and situate them somewhere beyond themselves. Dad is more likely to make sure his child is able to meet and overcome the challenges life is certain to bring.

In a more practical way, moms are motivated primarily by things from the outside world that could possibly confront or hurt their children: lightning, accidents, disease, teasing meanies, strange people, dogs in the neighborhood, and so on. They seek to protect their children from such contingencies. Dads—while not unconcerned with these dangers— take a different approach. They tend to focus on how their children will or will not be prepared for something harmful or challenging they might encounter in the world: a bully, being nervous around the opposite sex, fierce competition at baseball or soccer tryouts, and so forth.

Put as simply as possible: dad prepares; mom protects. Think about this and observe whether this is true in your family.

Because of dad's vantage point, he will tend toward helping children see themselves in relation to the larger world. This is critical, teaching how particular attitudes and behaviors bring certain consequences, both good and bad. Dads are more likely to teach both boys and girls how they can take control of their world to influence and shift a situation for the sake of their protection, dignity, and even gain. For example, dads are more likely to worry that their children won't grow up to contribute to society or experience the benefits of being a leader. They're thinking long-term. Moms are more likely to try to soften the immediate blows of hard-life realities on children out of a desire to protect.

SEEKING BALANCE

So which way is best, mom's or dad's? The answer to this question might depend on your perspective as a mom or dad. But as with nearly all of these male-female distinctions, our children benefit from both protection and preparation. These qualities provide children with essential comfort and care as well as confidence and preparation to face the outside world.

Our kids need both mom and dad for an essential balance. A sense of security is critical to a child's happiness and self-worth. Remember Michael, my childhood friend whose parents didn't communicate the slightest utterance of concern or protection for him? Instead of feeling free and independent, he felt as if he were worth no more than a single penny to his parents. They actually showed more thoughtfulness and concern for their dog.

That's a heavy message for a child. Care and protection build confidence and nurture a sense of being loved and valued. Yet the confidence that comes from being prepared to handle trouble and difficulties is necessary as well. Who is more appreciated in a group, on a team, or in a classroom: the person who shrinks from danger and difficulty or the one who knows how to handle it and does so skillfully?

While both preparation and protection provide necessary developmental goods, they also serve to balance each other out. A child who only knows how to stay away from danger might be safe from physical harm, but he'll be unprepared when he finds himself in a dicey situation. That's not good. At the same time, a child who is very confident about handling herself in every situation but doesn't have insight or wisdom in how to avoid such challenges in the first place isn't healthy either. A healthy young man or young woman has a good grasp on both ways in the face of threat. Avoidance and preparation are essential for a healthy sense of safety and security. And they both come from mom and dad.

This truth was curiously demonstrated some years ago in a *USA Today* feel-good feature on how "families come in all sizes and shapes" and no one type of family is right for everyone.

This particular feature family consisted of a lesbian couple, their male sperm donor live-in friend, his boyfriend, their little boy, and another one on the way. They all consider themselves a happy American family. Of course, this group probably wouldn't accept the information regarding gender roles in parenting that we've been exploring.

However, the journalist observing the ins and outs of this unique family's functioning asked if the adults ever butt heads on how to best raise the child. The biological father observed that the moms tended to pamper Alec too much: "When he falls down, she wants to rush over and make sure he is OK. I know he will be fine." This father, regardless of how much he might think he has set himself apart from so-called silly gender stereotypes, unwittingly is doing what fathers tend to do. He wants his boy to be given the opportunity to figure out and solve problems for himself, realizing he'll gain confidence and ability by such an exercise. These mothers want Alec to know they will always be there for him.

Unfortunately, little Alec gets shortchanged because the biological father said he keeps quiet and defers to the women on the matter because, after all, they are the legal parents. He's just the live-in sperm donor.[1]

Alec needs more from that man than his one-time deposit of fatherhood. But he doesn't get it, because this family thinks those silly gender stereotypes are for the *Leave It to Beaver* and *Father Knows Best* generation. However, their family is really more about what the adults want than what the boy needs.

This story reminds us of the irony that no matter how much we want to believe we can overcome the "narrow" boundaries of gender roles—with all these seemingly gender-free families where you need an org chart to tell who is who—nature is nagging and persistent. Once these folks think they have set themselves free from its hold, it creeps back up in a thousand different and unexpected ways.

The fact is, our children need their mothers to protect them from the dangers that lurk nearby, and they need their fathers to prepare them to handle those dangers.

———

I understand what you're saying about the differences between mom and dad. But I believe we do better by teaching our children that men and women are equal and both can do the parenting jobs that need to be done. Why can't this work?

The short answer is, because it doesn't work. Ample evidence of that comes from the large group of parents who for the last thirty years or so has tried to show that gender difference is only about body parts. Many think that sex differences are simply a result of cultural pressure and the effort of men to control women.

However, as such people try to live by these ideas, they find the issue a bit more complex. They learn that, as parents, they just can't help but act in sex-specific ways. Neither can their children. Their little girls will put their dump trucks down for a nap after the tea party with the airplane, pull-string power saw, and fire truck. And the boys will see how fast they can race their baby strollers down the driveway and if they can crash them at the finish line as an added bonus.

I believe we have to lose the idea that different means unequal. We don't operate this way in any other part of our lives. If I told you that sushi and Italian restaurants were *different* in important ways, you wouldn't ask what right I have to say one is *better* than the other. *Different* is not necessarily inferior or superior, so why should we act as though it is in the deeply meaningful and consequential areas that are so basic to who we are?

———

How do parents work it out when dad wants to teach the kids to do things mom thinks they might not be ready for?

This is an important question, and not just for children. It's also important for parents and their cooperation in parenthood and marriage.

Questions like this will force mom and dad to talk out the proper and healthy balance for their children. Moms and dads need to work this out together, with each giving the reasons for their convictions. They need to discuss their concerns in light of the particular abilities, weaknesses, temperaments, and attitudes of each of their unique children.

Moms and dads also need to be open to the reality that their spouse might have some God-given insight into the issue. Give-and-take is what helps parents navigate these areas of disagreement, as mom and dad see the value and wisdom in the other's perspective. This is much more healthy and productive than butting heads because you are set on your own way of parenting.

TWELVE

Your Child Is a Sexual Being

At age nine, Isabel, our youngest, is going through a *huge* daddy period where she can't get enough of me. She hugs me, follows me around, asks me questions, invites me to play games, and wants me to sit next to her on the couch to watch movies together. In her mind, her daddy couldn't possibly have anything else that needs doing other than just hanging out with her. I love it because I love her.

While this attraction and interest isn't completely gender based, it's not sex neutral either. The daddy-daughter relationship is very much at play and critical to her development. She's excited about me and my personality, but we'd be foolish to not recognize that she's also excited and curious about her male parent. She's learning (hopefully!) what a good and kind man is and learning she can expect such behavior and treatment from a man. I don't ever want her to be disappointed in that, not with me or any other men she develops meaningful relationships with—particularly boyfriends and eventually a husband.

Even though I've been through this phase of life with three other daughters and our son, I always surprise myself when my thoughts turn to their future spouses. Sometimes that thought leads to imagining my kids as parents, wondering what kinds of moms and dad they will make. Even more shocking is the realization that my own children are sexual beings. Yes, even though I research this kind of stuff for a living, I'm always a bit uneasy when I think of my own children as sexual beings.

THE SEXUALITY OF CHILDREN

As parents, we must realize that all children are sexually active. Even yours! At this point, you're probably wondering where this Stanton guy is coming from. You're thinking, *Are you insane? My child is twenty-three months old!*

Yes, I hear you. But it's true, and this statement is neither overstated nor idiotic. Of course, it might seem that way if your definition of *sexually active* is particularly narrow. However, that's like saying that people only learn if they sit in front of a teacher who is giving a lesson. That's one way of learning and maybe the most commonly recognized. But just as we are always learning, even when we're not aware of it, we are also sexually active far more often and much earlier in life than we appreciate. You see, to be human is to be a sexual creature.

What's more, our sexuality is *not* a consequence of the Fall, but a God-created, God-blessed, and God-commanded human experience. How many times have you heard in church that sexual engagement was the first command given to humanity? It most certainly was. God's Word is distinctly clear: Genesis 1:28.

And what are man's first recorded words in Scripture? They are

Adam's, upon seeing Eve, the woman who would complete him: "This is now bone of my bones and flesh of my flesh" (Genesis 2:23). Adam, the male, notices Eve, the female. He not only notices, but he's quite jazzed about her physicality—just as any other healthy man recognizes about his new bride. This isn't some base, fleshly, or carnal thought. Adam notices the God-created wonder of his wife. She notices the same about him. And God doesn't scold them.

He delights in this recognition, this first marital exchange of delight in seeing each other. Don't you think that Adam and Eve were sexually active from this very first moment, even if their thoughts and excitement hadn't yet turned toward consummation? Christianity teaches that we are sexual beings by design, not by flaw. So we must learn how to receive and care for this gift in God-honoring ways.

Our children, regardless of age and development, are sexually active because they are human. When our children start to nurse, it's not just about the milk. This act is as much about communion, closeness, and tenderness. As we've noted before, babies enjoy and receive comfort from the soft and tender flesh of momma. They learn to love her smell. On the other hand, daddy is stimulating. He is rougher, louder, and smells different. Remember, research consistently finds that babies as young as just a few weeks can detect the differences in mom and dad. In a way, this is one of their early lessons in sexuality. In fact, the basic distinction between male and female may provide their biggest lesson. All the other distinctions are details.

As you think about your developing child, consider how he or she is sexually active in this larger sense. This is important to be aware of. Is he or she fascinated with daddy's beard or facial stubble? Does your little boy sometimes play with his penis? Perhaps too often for your comfort? Have your children learned appropriate names for their "under their bathing suit" parts? What level of modesty do you show when changing your clothes, showering, or going to the bathroom in front of your children, and how old are they when you exercise this modesty? What are your kids' reactions when you and your spouse kiss in front of them? These are all ways in which our children develop understanding, insight, and values about sexuality.

Every one of us is sexually active, far more than we realize.

THE SEXUAL MARKETPLACE

At the same time, all parents should be thinking about sexual activity in the narrower definition we usually think of. The sexual economy—the give-and-take and negotiations of sexual exchange—that your children will participate in as they mature is largely lawless of late. In today's culture, for the most part, only one rule of thumb remains consistent: yes means yes and no means no. Get this settled and there is little anyone should say about your sexual business. Period. Everything else is fair game. Or so our culture suggests.

The sexual marketplace today operates on free-market principles beyond your imagination, and the ironic thing is that you were raised in a fairly open sexual culture, unless you were born before 1945 and came of age in the 1950s. Essentially, a hook-up culture has replaced a dating culture. This occurs at very young ages in certain demographic groups. There used be some sort of ritual for even the most sexually liberated young adult—involving an invitation for a date, plans for the boy to pick the girl up at her house, and then dinner or a movie or both—before going back to either one's apartment. The really naughty girls and boys might willingly engage after dinner in the backseat of the young man's car. Now, the only lead-up to a sexual encounter seems to be consuming enough alcohol to kill whatever inhibitions either partner has about hooking up with someone whose name they might not even know. Physically, this is a stunningly efficient system. No emotion, no preparation, no real connection, no call afterward. Any ongoing connection between sexually involved young men and women is more likely to be referred to as "friends with benefits" rather than "dating" or "going steady." Nothing more than two friends, relieving each other's sexual energy, like a close friend might regularly massage your back or help stretch your sore leg.

How do young people feel about this? Donna Freitas, a professor of religion at Boston University, has studied the sexual landscape on America's college campuses more closely than anyone. Her research, contained in her riveting book *Sex and the Soul,* reveals a heart-wrenching story. In fact, Freitas actually started her research because of the empty nature she sensed in this increasingly hook-up culture. In one of her classes years ago, she listened as her seniors had returned from spring break and spoke of all the fun and sexual experiences they'd enjoyed. The way these well-tanned and detoxing students told their tales, it was all great and proud news.

Then one sober voice spoke up, just like the little boy in the story of "The Emperor's New Clothes." She said that although she'd participated in the hook-up culture as she thought she was supposed to, she admitted to the class that she actually hated it. There was nothing good about it, from her perspective. To be honest, she said, it left her feeling depressed, degraded, and used. It felt as though her soul had been pulled out more and more with each careless interchange. Slowly, the other students' sentiments turned from bragging to honest regret. Amazing! Professor Freitas was stunned at the turn taking place in front of her. Her students began to admit aloud, "We're not happy with the hookup culture. We feel a constant pressure to do things that make us feel unsettled."

They began to ask as a group if they thought they could resist just doing what everyone else does and call their peers to something greater, more noble. Freitas explains how her students changed as they began to study the issue of human sexuality in more detail. Somewhere in between the readings and discussions, their dismay about campus hookups and the practice's "lack of romance took root and grew like a weed until they could no longer ignore it.… They wanted the right to demand more from their peers when it came to sex and relationships—more joy, more satisfaction, more commitment—and less sex. Maybe even no sex," she explained.[1] She was witnessing a small, new kind of sexual revolution.

While these kids weren't transformed into abstinence crusaders, they were questioning the status quo that compelled them to act in ways they actually hated. That's a start.

Interesting groups springing up on Ivy League campuses are unapologetically preaching and practicing abstinence. But their message is far from, "Just say no!" I've had the pleasure and honor of visiting some of these students at Princeton and Harvard. They are brilliant students, confident, engaging, and not all of them religiously motivated, although most are. They provide sophisticated explanations for why they believe saving sexual engagement for the security of marriage is wise. They draw from literature, philosophy, history, and theology. They put far more complex and intellectual thought into their positions for chastity than the hooker-uppers, whose only reason for their behavior is that they think that's what they're supposed to do.

All of this suggests that the latest generation of young adults is deeply dissatisfied with the removal of all sexual guardrails. As parents we must realize that one of the most enjoyable and fulfilling parts of our children's adult lives can be their sexual relationships. How can we not also understand that one of the most hurtful, shame-producing, violent, and degrading experiences in their adult lives could be their sexual relationships? Which story becomes each of our children's stories is deeply affected by their relationships and experiences with their mothers and fathers.

Perhaps the biggest contributor to either good or bad stories for our own kids regarding their future sexual relationships isn't whether they become masters of the *Kama Sutra* but how they view and value their own sex and sexuality as well as that of their future spouses. Sex is much less about technique and ability than it is about beliefs and the nature of the relationship in which the sexual exchange takes place.

What Matters in Sex

The largest, most sophisticated, truly scientific study of sexuality in America was published in the early 1990s. Coming out of the University of Chicago, this study looked at everything sexual. One of the most surprising findings revealed who had the most physically and emotionally satisfying sexual relationships. This last distinction is important because sex can be physically exciting "in the moment" yet emotionally disappointing, even destructive, in the long run. So looking at both is an important measure for satisfaction. Who did this research identify as the most sexually satisfied folks out there?

It wasn't the sexually adventurous types. In fact, the study found that, in general, sexual satisfaction decreased as the number of lifetime sexual partners increased. And later marital success and durability declined the longer one's premarital sexual résumé was.[2] The most sexually satisfied folks in your community are the couple down the street, married faithfully to each other for thirty-one years. They have four kids and drive the minivan with that busted headlight and a hubcap missing. Seriously! The researchers explain, "In real life, the unheralded, seldom discussed world of married sex is actually the one that satisfies people the most."[3] And among those who are married, those who came to their marriage with *no* prior sexual experience were more likely to report greater overall happiness than those who had previous sexual experience with other partners. What's more, married women were least likely to be forced to do something sexual by their partners, while the dating and cohabitants were most likely. Husbands are more likely to treat their wives with respect than daters and cohabitants, and wives are more successful in demanding that respect from their men than girlfriends are. This connects with what we observed earlier, that women, especially married women, know how to get men to behave.

What Boys and Girls Both Need to Know About Their Differences

At the proper age, our boys and girls need to understand what's unique about the bodies of the opposite gender and why God gave them these special and interesting gifts. Our children, both boys and girls, should know what their "private parts" are for and what purpose they serve. Why did God make them like this, and how do the two types of bodies, minds, and spirits work together?

Mothers and fathers each make distinctly different contributions to a child's developing understanding of gender. All is not equal on this particular front. Research shows that fathers tend to respond more significantly to their children as sex-distinct beings. Mothers treat both boys and girls more similarly.[4]

Put another way, dads stimulate more of the "boyness" in boys and the "girlness" in girls. This helps children understand that they are sex-distinct and that this distinction means something: in the way they do things and even what they will or won't do. At the same time, mothers don't emphasize these differences as starkly as dads do. This helps children know that sex difference is not their complete story. Both boys and girls learn important lessons by seeing and experiencing moms not make the distinctions that dads do. This helps our children not be so absolute in their differences. Both mom and dad provide a necessary balance by simply being mom and dad, and together in their different ways, they shape their children's healthy understanding of gender.

How Mom and Dad Together Teach Confident, Healthy Sexuality

As we've seen in countless ways, men and women are different. They eat and dress differently. They groom themselves differently. They get frustrated and impatient differently. They get over frustration and impatience differently. They have different dreams and desires, different motivations. As parents, dads do "man things" for the most part, and moms are more likely to do "woman things." Interesting how it works out that way.

Our little boys and girls learn about the habits, manners, quirks, and routines of both men and women by living with and observing the comings and goings, the doings and not doings of their moms and dads. Suzanne Frayser, a celebrated anthropologist in the study of gender distinction and sexuality across broad human cultures, explains that this male-female education by mothers and fathers is constant in all human societies:

> Each process complements the other. The boy can look at his father and see what he should do to be a male; he can look at his mother to see what he should *not* do to be a male. The importance of contrasts in gender roles and the specification of gender identity may be clues to the psychological importance of sexual differentiation in all societies.[5] (emphasis in the original)

Boys who grow up with warm and close connections with their fathers are more likely to develop a healthy masculine senses of self, compared to boys who don't have such relationships with their fathers due to absence or harshness.[6] Boys who grow up with close, affectionate, and affirming relationships with their mothers have a better sensitivity to and understanding of women. They're also more likely to be respectful and considerate of women in their lives as they grow and mature.

Girls who grow up close to affirming, warm, loving, and confident moms are more likely to be secure and healthy in their womanhood. Girls who grow up close to their fathers in loving and affirming relationships are more likely to be confident around boys and men as they grow. They're much less likely to be manipulated by immature and ill-intentioned boys. Consider the following:

Girls who are close to their fathers...

- have healthier relationships with boys in adolescence and men in adulthood. These girls learn from their dads how proper men should act and therefore know what to expect. And their dad-given confidence gives them the foundation to expect nothing less than the right things from the boys and men in their lives.

- have a healthy familiarity with the world of men. They don't wonder how a man's facial stubble or strong chest feels or what it's like to be hugged and held by strong arms. While still being moved by these things, finding them mysterious and exciting, they tend to simply appreciate and be less intrigued or obsessed by these manly qualities.

- have an emotional security based on this familiarity with men, which boosts their safety from exploitation. They don't have an unhealthy need for male physical affection and attention.

Girls who are close to their mothers...

- have a healthier confidence in their femininity because they've had it modeled for them by a confident woman in relation to her husband and others in the community. These girls don't have as much to prove, because they know who they are and what womanhood is.
- know how to carry themselves and respect their bodies. They exhibit a healthy balance between prudishness and immodesty, are comfortable being women, and express their femininity and womanly power in natural and healthy ways.
- are less likely to be petty and catty based on this confidence. Their confidence and security allow them to be more gracious and giving to others, especially women, rather than seeing them as competitors.

I recently went to an all-night breakfast place with Livvy and her fellow cast members after their final play performance. I was going to sit elsewhere and give her some space with her friends, but she insisted I sit at her table with her. Wow, my teenage daughter wanted me to sit with her in the midst of all her friends! I asked her if she was sure, and she said she was. It was fascinating to watch her with her friends. I was struck with how kind she was to everyone and how much the others valued her. She interacted with each peer (boys and girls) as if they were the most important person in her world, and it was obvious she truly believed that what they had to say was important. She was so comfortable doing so. This confidence in her kindness came from her mom, and it was wonderful for her dad to see.

Similarly, what comes from healthy relationships between boys and their parents? Consider these points.

Boys who are close to their fathers…

- are more secure with their masculine qualities and strengths and less likely to be violent. Gang activity, bullying, and pornography are less likely to be an attraction. These boys know they are men and don't need to display their masculinity, seek attention, or fight as hard for respect. They're not as likely to need to be noticed for toughness or violence.

- know how to channel their male strength and power in positive ways through hard work, discipline, leading well, and serving others.

- are more prepared to deal with the challenges of life because of their greater confidence in who they are as men as well as their greater overall problem-solving skills and abilities.

- demonstrate respect toward women because they've had training from dad in his mistakes and oversights in his relationship with mom. They better learn how to treat women and honor them.

Boys who are close to their mothers…

- are more secure and comfortable around girls, knowing what behaviors and attitudes are appropriate with females. They don't have to work to impress because they know how. They know what women want, and they've practiced proper behavior, been corrected at times, and gained experience.

- are less likely to manipulate girls.

- show more sensitivity to emotion and emotional cues from women because they've gained an understanding of women's expectations and what good men do in these relationships.

Fathers and Mothers Teach Kids to Respect— and to Expect Respect from—the Opposite Sex

Fact: A married mother and father are substantially less likely to be abusive to each other or their children than couples who are either dating or merely cohabiting.[7]

Boys raised with fathers are more likely to be good husbands, because they can emulate their fathers' successes and learn from their failures. Boys with good moms and dads are dramatically less likely to exploit women sexually. For one, they have a greater respect for women, given to and demanded by mom. They also have less need for collecting sexual conquests, because they have gained a healthy and secure sense of masculinity from dad's example and instruction.

Girls with caring, involved, married fathers are more likely to select for themselves good suitors and husbands, because they have a good standard by which to judge all candidates. Fathers themselves help weed out bad candidates, even more than mom does. Girls learn from their fathers how a woman should be treated because of his love, care, and respect for both mother and daughter. These girls also don't have the unhealthy ache of needing the attention of a man, any man. In addition, girls whose confidence has been nurtured by mom and dad find they don't have to be cunning and manipulative in their own relationships and marriage. These girls are likely to have learned from both mom and dad, in different ways, how to ask for what they want, including when to insist and when to compromise.

By contrast, girls who grow up without a confident mother or a protective and caring father are the easiest marks for sexually exploitive boys and men. These girls haven't gained womanly confidence from their mothers on how to be treated respectfully by men. Clinical psychologist Evelyn Bassoff, in her book on raising healthy women, recognizes,

If our daughters are to flower, they need optimal growing
conditions: Almost always this means being lovingly cared for
by mother and father. It is from her mother that a girl learns to
be a woman; it is from her father that she learns what to expect
from men in the way of love and respect.[8]

Over the last few decades, numerous studies have consistently shown
that young boys and girls raised by both their moms and dads are substantially less likely to be sexually active in their teen years, compared to
their peers in single-parent or stepfamilies.

Noted sociologist Scott Coltrane found that throughout many diverse cultures, when men and women both participated in family work as
a team, these cultures were much more likely to have a higher view of and
respect for women and less likely to exclude them from public activities
and leadership than when compared to more father-absent societies.[9]

Mothers and fathers, working together in the parenting task, help
the next generation of humanity develop a healthy understanding of who
they are sexually. This is a key part of our human development.

———

You quoted the research where married people say their sex lives are more
satisfying than those who aren't married or those who have many sex
partners. Why do you think that's the case?

This question goes right to the heart of what we are as human beings and
what sexuality is. C. S. Lewis explains it well in his book *Mere Christianity:* "The monstrosity of sexual intercourse outside marriage is that those
who indulge in it are trying to isolate one kind of union (the sexual) from
all the other kinds of union which were intended to go along with it and

make up the total union."[10] A Christian view of human sexuality is all about context—making sure we don't separate some parts of ourselves from all the others that make us a complete being. *The Message,* Eugene Peterson's paraphrase of the Bible, states it this way:

> There's more to sex than mere skin on skin. Sex is as much spiritual mystery as physical fact. As written in Scripture, "The two become one."… We must not pursue the kind of sex that avoids commitment and intimacy, leaving us more lonely than ever—the kind of sex that can never "become one." There is a sense in which sexual sins are different from all others. In sexual sin we violate the sacredness of our own bodies, these bodies that were made for God-given and God-modeled love, for "becoming one" with another. (1 Corinthians 6:16–18)

I explain it this way in a previous book, *My Crazy Imperfect Christian Family:*

> The human sexual embrace, this most intimate and ultimate of all human giving and vulnerability, ought to take place in a union of total and permanent surrender of two people. That's what marriage is: both the public and personal dedication of a man and woman to forsake all others and give themselves fully—body, mind, and spirit—to another as a total gift of self.…
>
> That's why sex outside marriage is a monstrosity. Extramarital sex dissects us at our deepest level, giving out one part of us without giving all the rest intended to go with it. It's not what we're made for.
>
> Where did we ever get the idea that we can separate our bodies from our minds and spirits and that our bodies could do

whatever they like without consequence for the rest of our being? This is why the sexual revolution has been such a dehumanizing failure, diminishing our God-given humanity in painful ways.... We can't connect ourselves with someone sexually without connecting all the rest of our being....

Only the sexual embrace *within marriage* mirrors the nature of the Trinitarian relationship in creation. In the ideal, it's loving, permanent, exclusive, and self-giving. Premarital and extramarital sex can't mirror this reality. This is why it's not surprising research shows that faithfully married people enjoy the deepest levels of sexual satisfaction.[11] (emphasis in the original)

Marriage provides the emotional, spiritual, and physical safety that allows us to give ourselves away to each other with complete abandon and to trust each other. That is why sex is so fulfilling only in the protective and freeing harbor of marriage.

———

Can you explain why, when fathers are involved more in family life, women are afforded greater influence and leadership in those cultures?

Scott Coltrane's research, which we just touched on, is important work and is also backed up by other studies. There are a few reasons the male-female domestic and cultural dynamic contributes to the better treatment of women.

First is a hidden but real impact of marriage upon men: it lowers their testosterone levels, making them less aggressive and competitive. There is indication that men's testosterone levels also decrease as they become fathers, the natural settling effect of being linked permanently to a woman in marriage and children in parenthood.[12] This makes men less inclined to elbow competitors, male or female, out of community leadership positions.

Second, as men live with and work alongside women, they come to trust them, to appreciate their unique giftings and insights. This makes the men less intimidated by women moving into leadership positions and therefore less likely to discourage or hinder them. These men also become more confident in the abilities of female peers to do a good job.

Third, married women develop a soft and indirect influence over their husbands (as well as other men) through gentle and strategic prodding, encouragement, and expectations. This has a positive benefit, not just for the wives, but for all women in the community who benefit from men becoming more comfortable following the lead and influence of women in measured and particular ways.

THIRTEEN

How Mom and Dad Raise Kids Who Care

Do you remember the commercial a few years ago featuring the very cute kids, in one frame after another, declaring statements like these?

- "When I grow up, I wanna file *all* day."
- "I wanna climb my way up to middle management!"
- "I wanna be a yes-man!"
- "When I grow up, I wanna be underappreciated."

The Monster.com commercial was an effective attention grabber because no child or parent holds such dreams for the future.

Think about all the objectives we have as parents. They don't vary all that much from person to person and culture to culture. Anthropologists are seldom blown away by their research, exclaiming, "Wow, do you know what they raise kids for in *this* culture? We've never seen this in any other culture known to humanity!"

Most parents throughout time and the world have pretty much the same objectives. They want their children to be obedient, grow, mature, become happy and independent, and experience some significant measure of material success. Parents desire that their children become educated in the ways, wisdom, and knowledge of the culture. Parents hope their kids will become leaders or make some sort of important contributions to the community. Moms and dads want their children to be strong, secure, and loved. Mothers and fathers want their kids to find spouses and have good, kind, keen children themselves. They want to see their children grow up to be happy, well liked, talented. Most want their children to share and practice the faith of their family. Can you imagine any half-decent parent in the world not wanting these things for their children?

But perhaps your most primary, most basic goal as a parent is to share your love. You sense how much joy and meaning your life will gain through having, loving, and raising a child. And you look forward to seeing that child grow, in turn, into a compassionate, caring, self-sacrificing adult.

Let's look at how children learn these important qualities—empathy, compassion, and selflessness—from their moms and dads. You might be surprised by how this develops in our children.

DEVELOPING AN OTHERS-CENTERED LIFE

If you had to guess where children are more likely to develop empathy—concern for the well-being of others—who would you say is more likely to be the source, mom or dad? Mom, right? As we discussed before, mom is the feeler, while dad is the doer. She is the more sensitive one. Dad is more pragmatic.

Surprisingly, *dad* is the right answer! Child-development research over the past forty years strongly points to a father's profound influence in developing empathy. Probably the most sophisticated study on the subject was a longitudinal examination initiated in the mid-1950s with conclusions published in 1990. The study's authors found it "quite astonishing" that the strongest factor in children demonstrating greater levels of empathic concern in their thirties and beyond was a father's participation in their early care. The study's authors explain that this factor of paternal child care carried more weight than the three strongest maternal factors *combined*! The twenty-six-year study concludes, "These results appear to fit with previous findings indicating that pro-social behaviors such as altruism and generosity in children were related to active involvement in child care by fathers."[1]

How can this be? It makes great sense if we look deeply at what fathers do for their children. Think about aggression in children. Which parent most effectively lessens the level of aggression? Moms might demonstrate less violent and physical behavior than fathers and be more concerned with justice and fairness, but children with involved fathers develop greater self-regulation and control and learn to "act out" less. A number of studies show that "fathers may be particularly important for helping very young children gain control over intense emotions."[2] Moms help their kids get in touch with their emotions. Fathers help their children manage them.

The management of an individual's own emotions is the primary foundation for reading and understanding the emotions of others. When it's all about you, it's hard to consider others. When it's not all about you, concern for others comes naturally. Let's look at this in more detail.

How Fathers Teach Empathy

Consider the differences we've been exploring between moms and dads. John Snarey, professor of human development at Emory University, conducted a four-decade study on how child development is influenced by fathers. His insight confirms what we know about the importance of play and safety: mothers and fathers have different orientations; therefore, they have different ways of orienting children in relation to the world.

As we've already discovered, mothers view the world in relation to the child, asking, "What out there could hurt him?" Fathers see their child in relation to the world, asking, "What out there should my child be prepared for?" This is critical for empathic development. Snarey explains that fathers are more likely to build concern and empathy in their children not by directly teaching and demonstrating but by encouraging their children to recognize situations in the world around them. Dads further urge their children to be prepared to meet the world and change it for the better. This influence applies to both simple and complex things.[3]

We can see how actions of empathy and concern develop when a child learns from dad to be aware of the environment and do the right thing relative to that environment. Picture a child, boy or girl, playing on the playground. Someone is teasing another child because he's too scared to climb high enough to go down the slide. Our hero child, as influenced by dad, sees this interaction and senses the other child's pain because dad has, without even realizing it, taught his child to be aware of his surroundings and do something about it. This is what men do. Just as dad teaches a child to be mindful of possibly dangerous people or situations and take the proper actions, he also teaches awareness of the feelings and predicaments of others. Through dad's influence, his child is more aware of the situation and has the confidence, conviction, and encouragement to do something about it.

This outward-looking view helps our children naturally learn not only to be mindful of others but also to do something about it. This sense of empathy and compassion also results from principled leadership that dads are more likely to teach through indirect means, such as stopping to help someone with a flat tire or helping the neighbors fix their fence. Of course, mom cares about others too. But her ways of helping others are typically more subtle, like consoling a friend or working behind the scenes.

I remember when I was young, our father had my siblings and me pick up trash along a strip of land beside our house that belonged to no one. I remember wondering why we'd work so hard to care for something that wasn't ours. He explained that we were showing pride for our neighborhood and also serving our neighbors by doing this simple task of regularly picking up trash along this strip of land. This was about "doing" for my dad, but it was also about "doing" for the common good.

Another time in my childhood, when I was much younger, my brother and I dressed up like clowns. Our mom made these cool little costumes for us, and we took part in a play my father and some of his friends from church put on for kids at an orphanage. In the play, my father and his friends portrayed hapless construction workers building a house. They entertained the children by being wacky and confused as they "worked." I remember the kids laughing at these grown men being so dumb and knuckleheaded. As one of the preconstructed walls was brought on stage as part of the house, my brother and I were hidden behind it. This allowed us to get into the house unseen and "magically" come out when it was finished. As we popped out to the children's surprise, we got to throw candy and little trinkets to them. Todd and I learned how fun it could be to do something nice for others.

Additionally, fathers teach a development of compassion and consideration through rough play. How does this help? Ross Parke, a pioneer in the research on father involvement with children, explains that rough play teaches the child to read the cues of the partner to see if the play is too rough or not exciting enough and to regulate accordingly to make it most enjoyable. As we've discussed, dad's play has a greater range of excitement and arousal higher than the more modulated play of mothers with their children.[4] This means that dad is more likely to demonstrate to or encourage his kids to be aware of how the activity is going relative to others and to make necessary adjustments—which he does without even thinking about it.

Parke also finds that having involved and warm fathers participating in positive play with a son or daughter tends to increase the child's peer popularity, because the child will exhibit greater sensitivity to others.

WHAT ABOUT MOMS?

So do mothers play any role in helping their children develop caring, prosocial attitudes and behaviors? Of course! Moms teach through their influence. They actually help shape and influence fathers to be more effective teachers of compassion.

Research shows that fathers who are harsh, dominating, and overly corrective have children who aren't as likely to be sympathetic.[5] Mothers play an important role in helping fathers deal more consistently and graciously with their children, which improves dad's ability to pass on lessons of compassion. In other words, fathers who are strongest in indirectly teaching their kids empathy and compassion are being influenced to do so in many ways by mom. While this seems indirect or complex, it's actually a very connected team effort.

A nurturing give-and-take between child and dad is critical, but mom helps shape this in real and necessary ways. Like so many things mothers do, the impact is clearly there, but it's more subtle and soft.

Professor David Popenoe explains the importance of this topic for our children's healthy development:

Nothing is more important for the development of prosocial children and teenagers than the teaching of empathy—the ability to experience the thoughts, feelings, and attitudes of another person. In other words, in order to have law-abiding, cooperative, and compassionate adults, we must first teach them as children to cultivate feelings of empathy.[6]

Mom and dad work together, in very different and even counterintuitive ways, to provide this essential quality in their children as they grow to be good, desirable, and appreciated adults.

———

My experience is that men are actually more tone-deaf to the feelings of others, to what's going on around them. They can be so focused on what they're doing that they completely miss cues that their help is needed in getting things done around the house.

This is an interesting observation, and there's some truth to it. Yet it doesn't undercut what we just explored in this chapter. Good men are taught that gentlemanliness requires them to be aware of others and make sure that all are cared for. I am struck by this in a friend of mine, Jeff Kemp, former Seattle Seahawks quarterback and son of football great Jack Kemp. Jack clearly taught his boys that strength comes through serving and considering the lives of others, and Jeff displays this in inspiring ways, especially for minorities. I've seen it in our work together.

While the general empathy that children learn from their fathers might not be as sharply attentive as what Jeff learned from his father, our kids indeed do learn it from their fathers. Often they learn it less by dad's example of being attentive to lending a hand and more by observing how dad considers their environment and takes the lead to make a change when things aren't working well.

Of course, dads do need to be more mindful and deliberate to make sure they offer this kind of sensitivity and leadership at home, particularly because, as we've learned, men tend to place more focus on what's going on "out there" in the greater community and world.

FOURTEEN

Gender Differences: The Basis for a Healthy Family

Here's an irony for you: one of the hardest things in my married life and role as a husband has been realizing I am married to a woman. No, I never mistake my sweet bride for a man.

What I've had a hard time realizing is that not only is my wife a different person than I am, but as a woman she looks at life, values things, and gets motivated, angered, bored, excited, and bothered by different things than I do. She rejoices and thrills differently than I do. She gets jazzed and depressed by different things. Too many times I expect her to have the same actions, reactions, conclusions, and feelings about something as I do. We love each other so much and have so much in common, so how could she be so different?

Jackie struggled in the same way with me. We were very similar as best friends in high school and later as spouses. Yet we are very different as male and female. This might be one of the greatest paradoxes of humanity and marriage. Think about this in your own marriage and family:

- Your engagement was tailored so that it had the deepest impact on whom?
- Your wedding ceremony clearly had the fingerprints of which spouse all over it?
- Perhaps the décor and design of your first house or apartment was a joint effort, but someone likely played a more dominant role. Who was it?
- What about the first car you bought together? Who was the primary decision maker on that?
- If you've made any recreational investments—a boat, a camper, a cabin, an RV—was the decision prompted by one partner's greater encouragement over the other's?
- When you started the process of growing your family in earnest—whether through getting pregnant or pursuing adoption—did you both come to that conclusion at exactly the same time, or did one of you have a greater influence on the other? Who was the initiator?

Often, husbands and wives hold different feelings, convictions, and ideas about a number of things. Marriage involves working out those differences in a cooperative way of mutual regard. Most married couples find this process to be more difficult than they imagined. Men and women will engage in discussion and debate in an effort to influence the other in very different ways. Does this hold true in your marriage?

The Fundamental Reality of Marriage

In these pages, you've likely noted many areas in which you and your spouse struggle as you raise and train your children together. Do you both always agree on what new things your child should try and when? Do you agree on discipline? Can one sometimes see things too rigidly while the other seems too permissive?

Here's a fundamental reality of marriage, and it is what makes marriage an important universal human institution. You are married to a creature who is similar to you but one who is also different in a vital way: he or she comes from the other team. This is what attracted you to each other. Because of this, you each view life differently—and your family needs both perspectives.

When I say that your spouse is very different than you, I'm not talking about personality or temperament. One of you might like the mountains while the other likes the beach; or maybe one is extroverted, the other introverted. Instead, I'm saying that marriage and parenting work because of the much deeper human and essential differences between male and female. These differences present great challenges as well as rich blessings. Your very existence is a tribute to what a blessing those differences can be, for without them you don't exist.

Healthy marriages and parenting rely in great part on the profound differences in the two partners' fundamental sex- and gender-based wiring, views, passions, values, and perspectives.

These are no small differences in the life of any family. God designed these differences to make us into better people. It's why all cultures—regardless of their differences in religion, customs, and law—have marriage, because marriage is the way men and women make each other better, happier, safer, and more influential in the community. Marriage is powerful precisely because it accomplishes this as no other human institution can.

The Truths That Shape Generations

Parenting brings both great joys and challenges that deeply enrich our lives as well as those of our spouse, our extended family, and our children—in large part because male and female are different. My prayer for you is that you have gained a deeper, more colorful appreciation for the essential contributions you make to the growth and maturity of your children. And that you know you do this simply by being the unique, gender-distinct parent God created you to be as you cooperate with another gender-distinct parent in raising gender-distinct children. Researching and writing this book has truly helped me in marriage and parenting with my and our children's treasure, Jacqueline.

I want to conclude with a very personal story that illustrates how living out our lives as sex-distinct beings—usually without our even being aware of it—impacts and shapes those around us in profound ways. This story involves my father's early life, what shaped him, and how that inevitably shaped his marriage to my mom and his raising of my four siblings and me. We lost my dad quite suddenly just over two years ago to a stroke, and I'd like to honor him by sharing his story.

Much of my father's boyhood wasn't known to my siblings and me until the last few years. The day after my mother died, I was able to spend what turned out to be a very special day alone with my father. I probably learned more about him that day than all the previous days of my life combined.

He wanted to go through all of their old photographs, looking for pictures of my mother to use in her memorial. Together he and I sorted through an old dusty briefcase, filled with photos that I'd *never* seen before. What I found most interesting were old pictures of my dad when he was a young boy. Prior to this day, his wedding pictures were the youngest I'd ever seen him in any photos. We knew nearly nothing of my dad's boyhood. The only thing he ever told us about it was his love of baseball.

"Who is this?" I asked him. He took the picture and looked at it carefully, as if he needed to think about who the people were. Of course he knew, but he was just taking in the images he hadn't seen in decades.

He answered me, "Why, that's me when I was little, with your grandpa and my sister."

Wow. I knew my dad had a sister, but I'd never seen her, even in pictures. He told me she was about twelve years older than he was and that she had left home when he was very young. He had no other stories of her or connection whatsoever. She was a phantom to us.

We continued working our way through the stash of photos, which took about three hours. Then, because my dad and I were in the house alone and his heart was obviously softened by the fresh loss of his wife, I told him that I didn't know much about his boyhood and wondered if he could tell me about it with these photos. I remembered his father, as he came around a few times when we were all very young, but I really only recalled enough to know that my grandfather existed and not much else. My father's mother had died when he was only two years old. I knew that my grandpa and dad lived by themselves in Washington DC.

My father started to tell me a specific story, describing how they moved around town often, from rented apartment to rented apartment every eight to twelve months. Dad didn't explain why; maybe these were things he thought I didn't need to know. He always felt he needed to shield us from unpleasant truths and never could appreciate that his boys had grown into men and could actually handle the truth, as gritty as it might be. My grandfather and dad didn't move so often because they grew antsy for new neighborhoods. My grandfather probably drank, perhaps didn't work much, or gambled away money or spent it in a manner fitting what my dad told me next.

As my dad explained that day at his dining room table—again, trying to shield his forty-something son—my grandpa "was quite a ladies' man," and he spent a great deal of time and money at the "men's store" buying nice clothes and suits. He made it sound as if my grandpa was Dean Martin, but I knew he was a blue-collar man who worked with his hands. My dad returned to the specific story and one particular day he wanted to describe to me.

On this day more than sixty-five years earlier, his father came out of the men's shop in downtown Washington and walked out into the street to get into his car. At that moment, a dump truck ran a red light, slammed into another car, and sent that car straight for my grandfather. It smashed and pinned him up against his own car. He was seriously injured and rushed to the hospital, where he was stabilized and would stay for the next few months. I wondered, *Why had I never heard this before? Not from my dad or my mom. How much of this had she known?*

My dad then related how he came home from school and playing baseball that evening and didn't find his father there. This wasn't strange, because his dad frequently didn't come home until late in the evening. So as a little fifth grader, my dad scrounged up something for dinner and ate it by himself as he did so many nights. He finished his homework, and when bedtime came he went to bed alone. He woke up the next morning expecting his father to have returned. But the apartment was empty. So my dad simply did what he did every day. He got himself ready and went to school, assuming and hoping his dad would come home that night. This went on for two or three days, and the days stretched into weeks. No one told my dad what had happened to his father, and my grandpa apparently didn't think to let anyone know. My dad only knew to do what he did every day: take care of himself. Only when someone finally reported to social services, expressing concern about this little boy coming and going to school with no supervision, did my dad find out what happened.

My goodness! Interestingly, he shared this story with me as if he were talking about a disappointing childhood vacation. He told it with no real emotion or the slightest recognition of how profound it was. This was one of the most revelatory moments of my entire life.

Sitting at the table with him at that moment is when I realized exactly why my dad had always been so emotionally stoic and protected. *How could he not be?* In those days and weeks, he gained the script that would be his life story: he only had himself to depend on; *there was no one else.* As a result, he could never afford to make himself vulnerable to anyone—not his children or his wife. He only had one enduring, close male friendship we can remember.

In fact, his last night on this earth is marked by this truth. He was a remarkably healthy and strong man, very active and fit. But on this evening, he felt that he was having a stroke and took what he thought was the appropriate action: he drove himself to the hospital! Calling an ambulance would have been "too much of a fuss" for my dad, not to mention requiring him to depend on someone else. So he handled it himself. He made it to the hospital parking lot but collapsed on the way into the building. Someone found him on the lawn near the emergency room entrance. The sprinklers had come on, and he just lay there, soaked and unconscious, near death.

The next day, May 1, 2008, William Edward Stanton died. I was the last one to say good-bye to him at the funeral home, as my brothers were able to see him just before he died. I never got to see my mom before or after she died, so it was important for me to see my father. It was meaningful for me, as the last one to see him, to be the one to take off his wedding ring and sign the legal papers confirming his identity. As the oldest son, I was honored to be the one who closed out his very sad life. I'm not sure who the first person to touch him at his birth was. I bet his mom was there, but I had no idea if his dad was there, proud to hold his first and only son (that we knew of). But I was the last one to touch him, to hold his hands, to rub his beard and stroke the short white hair on his head. I was his first son, and I turned the last page of the book that was his life.

As I stood there before him, I realized that I had never touched my father like this in my whole life. The most intimate we ever got was when I wrestled him as a boy. Now, as I saw him lying there lifeless with his eyes closed, it was the first time I had ever seen him content, at peace, and vulnerable. He wasn't striving to be good enough anymore. He didn't have to protect himself. If my dad had a life script, this was it. He didn't have to prove his worth anymore, and I was happy for him.

I hugged him and his cold, hard body. I told him his long, difficult struggle was over. He could now finally rest, received into the arms of the One who takes us not because of what we do but because of whose we are. I had this peace about my father because he loved and was learning to trust Jesus.

This was the first time—at age forty-six—that I felt like a man in my father's presence. And it was good that I was taking care of him, that he would finally allow someone to care for him.

After Dad's death, my brother Todd took a trip to the Northeast to visit his godmother, whom he hadn't seen since he was very young. She and her husband, now deceased, were childhood friends of my father. My brother knew she had a deep connection and first-person witness to our dad's early life. He wanted to hear her stories now that our father was gone.

She told Todd that she was glad he had come to visit, as she could now tell him things about our dad that she wouldn't while he was living—such as the first day she ever saw him. She was sitting at her desk in a Catholic grade school in a working-class neighborhood of Washington. A nun came in with a young ragamuffin boy in tow, whispered briefly to the nun in charge of the class, and left the boy with her. This nun tapped her pointer on the desk soundly and then announced, "Boys and girls, I want you to welcome a new boy to our class. His name is Billy Stanton, and he's a charity case we have to take in. So please help him learn the rules of our class. Now, Billy, go find a desk."

My father had come to this school after being taken into the care of social services while his father was still in the hospital. Todd's godmother said she never felt more sad or sorry for anyone than she did for that young boy at that moment, a boy who was officially judged and presented as a "charity case." She said he would come to school every day with his single set of white shirt and blue trousers as clean and pressed as a young boy could get them. Yet although his own meticulous efforts were obvious, he never looked really taken care of. She said from that moment on there was not a boy or man she respected more because of what he had overcome and how he made so much of his life from so little.

We'd never known any of this, and it was good for my siblings and me to hear from Todd, who got emotional as he told us. We just assumed our father was a hard man. Now we knew he had to fight his way into manhood, quite literally much of the way. He had lost most of his teeth and wore dentures all his adult life. He told us he lost them when he got elbowed in a rough basketball game. Todd's godmother explained tenderly, "Todd, I can tell you this. Billy didn't lose his teeth in a basketball game." It never occurred to us that that would have been *some* game!

My father gave me much. But there was also much he didn't give me because he didn't have it himself. These deficits from both his mother and father caused me to struggle greatly and to doubt myself deeply as I grew into manhood. Curiously, many of my successes and failures flow from this. But my dad couldn't give me what he didn't have. I've realized in these last two years that whatever I received of value from my father was a miracle and a testament to God's gracious hand upon me.

These experiences shaped him as a man, as a husband, and as a father. They shaped my mother as a wife and mother. They shaped my sister, Terry, as a wife and mother. They shaped my brothers and me as husbands and fathers.

To be human is to be gendered. As male or female, we are shaped—for better or worse—by a male and female who were shaped—for better or worse—by a male and female. This is the center of the human story, and it means the choices we make in living out our masculinity or femininity matter profoundly, especially in our marriage and our parenting. They touch everyone around us.

Are Men and Women Really Different? Consulting the Sciences

Good parents are good students. If you're one of those students who wants to earn extra credit by digging a little deeper into this topic, here's your opportunity to explore some of the interesting scientific data that exists for real, consequential differences between men and women.

In large measure, this is what *Secure Daughters, Confident Sons* has tried to answer, specifically how these differences play out in the family and why it is important for parenting, healthy child development, and marriage. I believe it's a fascinating topic.

In this appendix, I provide additional information that points to the important gender differences in men and women. Again, I want to stress that *different* certainly does not mean *unequal* or *inferior*. Even distinguished professor Alice Eagly of Northwestern University, a self-described "feminist psychologist," has found that these documented sex differences in behavior and personality do not cast womanhood in a bad light at all. Her investigations confirm what many of us have recognized: "the stereotype of women is more positive overall than the stereotype of men, at least in contemporary samples of U.S. and Canadian college students." She states that she is comforted by the fact that the sex differences documented in the literature "do not tell a simple tale of female inferiority."[1]

As you read on, please keep in mind that *different* doesn't mean *inferior*. Different means different—think *unique* if that helps—and many of these female and male differences show us how important, vital, and necessary both male and female are for society and the family. Each has essential qualities, strengths as well as weaknesses, that the other doesn't have.

In other words, men and women need each other, and this is the first human truth.[2]

MALE AND FEMALE ARE MALE AND FEMALE ALL OVER THE WORLD

Contrary to what some believe, differences between male and female are not just found in the U.S., Canada, Europe, or other developed nations. Investigations conducted in the last decade show that even though some specifics vary from culture to culture, clear and significant and essential differences between males and females are universal.

Across diverse cultures, scientists find that the tasks and activities performed interchangeably by male and female range from 0 percent to only 35 percent of general human activity.[3] Most of the work in all cultures has clear gender-based distinctions, which indicates that every culture establishes and shares common work on the basis of who is male and who is female. This is remarkable.

In fact, these cross-cultural studies are more interested in *why* sex distinctions exist in behaviors, expectations, personality, and divisions of labor rather than *whether* they exist, because they are clearly present across cultures. Eagly and her colleague conclude "that biology, social structure, and the environment interact reciprocally to produce the sex-typed roles" of men and women in communities.[4]

Another universal feature of social organization across cultures is found in parents and caregivers guiding both boys and girls in "sex appropriate" ways as they grow in their personal and social development. You cannot find a culture where what makes a girl a girl or a boy a boy is dramatically different from other cultures. The universal commonalities are what allow even an unobservant or uneducated member of one culture to go anywhere in the world and easily figure out which are the women and which are the men. In other words, no one has ever gone to a strange, new land and asked, "Now tell me, which ones are the guys here?"

MEN AND WOMEN SEEK CERTAIN KINDS OF MATES

Cross-cultural data on mate selection yield some interesting scientific findings. What do males and females report as being important in selecting a prospective long-term mate? If male and female are largely similar, wouldn't these desirable qualities be similar as well? And if gender difference is merely a cultural phenomenon, then these mate-preference qualities would vary from culture to culture. So what do we find?

A sophisticated examination of eighteen different mate-preference characteristics across thirty-seven different cultures on six continents and five islands, involving nearly ten thousand males and females (86 percent of them unmarried and looking) found marked differences between the priorities of men and women. Women around the world consistently are more likely to give a higher ranking to "social status and financial resources" as a leading desirable mate quality than men do. Care to guess what men look for? The researchers explain:

> These sex differences indicate that, consistent with previous work, women around the world value dependability, stability, education, and intelligence in a long-term mate more than do men. Conversely, men more than women value in potential mates their good looks, health, and a desire for home and children.[5]

I find this deeply interesting. Women and men engaged in spouse selection are *similarly different* across a wide diversity of cultures! This holds true among cultures profoundly separated from one another geographically and ideologically. If women are gold diggers and men seek trophy wives, they do so universally. But if women want a good man to depend on, care for, and protect them, and men want a good woman to start and raise a family with, they do so universally.

Anthropologist Kim Hill conducted ethnographic research among a preliterate, hunter-gatherer tribe in Paraguay. Hill was interested in finding out what kind of men the women there preferred as husbands. He spoke to a member of the Ache tribe named Achipura, asking what kind of man could easily get a wife, what kind most women would desire and look for. This was an easy question for Achipura: "He had to be a good hunter." Hill asked if this was most important, to which his interviewee responded, "No, not just a good hunter. A good hunter could find a wife, but a man needed to be strong."

Hill asked Achipura to clarify "strong." "Do you mean a man who could beat up others in a club fight?"

Achipura responded correctively: "No, women don't like those men.

Women don't like men who love to hit others. I mean a strong man. One who would walk far to hunt, one who would carry heavy loads. I mean a man who would work hard when everyone was tired, or build a hut when it was cold and rainy.... I mean a man who was strong. A man who could endure and not get tired."

Achipura explained that it didn't matter whether a man was large or small, but he had to be strong. Other qualities were important also, such as, "one who is handsome.... One who is nice and smiles and tells jokes.... A 'good man' is a man whom women love."[6]

Although Achipura's experience was rooted in a culture and community very different from yours, how much do the Ache standards for "a good man" vary from that of women in your part of the world? How different are they from how I describe men in this book?

These differences across cultures hold true when it comes to seeking physical attractiveness in a mate. Universally, 85 percent of men put this as the most important quality in a mate, while only 10 percent of women desired this as most important. Conversely, 80 percent of strong women indicated that "respect for partners' abilities and achievements" was very important in a partner, while only 30 percent of men reported this as important across cultures.[7]

THE MOOD FOR LOVE

Men and women are also different across cultures in their sexual appetites and desires. A study titled "Sociosexuality from Argentina to Zimbabwe" (Get it? From A to Z!), which explored forty-eight diverse nations, found that one gender is more sexually explorative than the other. As you might expect, women are universally less likely to report having sex with more than one partner in the past year than men were (22 percent versus 36 percent). Across these cultures, some monogamous and some nonmonogamous, 43 percent of women reported they foresee having sex with more than one partner in the next five years, compared to 62 percent of men who expected to.[8]

Findings from another major study—involving more than sixteen thousand people across fifty-two nations, six continents and thirteen islands, representing ten major world regions, with 119 scholars from around the world participating—support this stark male-female disparity in sexual appetite. The scholars explain, "Sex differences in the desire for sexual variety are culturally universal throughout these world regions." These sex differences were evident and consistent in many different ways as more measures were taken and analyzed. More than twice as many men as women desired to have more than one sexual partner in the next month, and even greater disparity existed between men and women in the "strongly- and moderately-seeking additional partners" categories.[9]

Other investigations found that when asked if they would have sex with someone they had known anywhere from only one hour to five years, men and women were only similar in the five-year mark, while men were far more willing to engage in sex with a partner they had known at each of the following intervals: an hour(!), a day, a week, a month, six months, a year, and two years. As if we needed further confirmation of the difference between men and women in this area, this question was posed across various and diverse cultures to men and women who were either married or in a relationship: "If the opportunity presented itself of having sexual intercourse with an anonymous member of the opposite sex who was as competent a lover as your partner but no more so, and who was as physically attractive as your partner but no more so, and there was *no* risk of pregnancy, discovery, or disease, and *no* chance of forming a more durable relationship, do you think you would do so?" (emphasis in original). Four times as many men said they "certainly would" as compared to women.[10]

Universally, men are less likely to remain faithful to their spouse or partner (60 percent) than women are (70 percent). The greatest divide between men and women in feelings about particular sexual situations was in response to this scenario: "No marriage, with freedom to have as many casual sex partners as you could attract."[11] But it is marriage that cultures use as the best mechanism to keep men faithful and focused on the family.

Additional gender differences concerning sexual experience were also examined in these various cross-cultural studies. Put on your best non-gender-stereotype thinking cap, and see if you can identify which is the correct answer—circle male, female, or both—for each of the following across all human cultures:

M/F/Both   Which gender is more likely to report feelings of guilt and being used following casual sex with different partners, even when reporting they weren't mistreated or lied to in the experience?

M/F/Both   Which shows more approval of casual sex?

M/F/Both   Regarding early sexual fantasies, who is far more likely to say their fantasies were initiated "in response to visual stimulus"?

M/F/Both   Who is far more likely to report their fantasies developed or occurred in the context of "a real or imagined romantic relationship"?

M/F/Both   Who demonstrates a greater frequency and earlier initiation of masturbation?

M/F/Both   Forty-five percent of which gender (compared to 6 percent of the other) reported they had sexual fantasies "many times a day"?

M/F/Both	Thirty-five percent of which gender said they had such fantasies "only once a week" (compared to only 8 percent of the other)?
M/F/Both	Which gender's fantasies were more sexually explicit, focused on body parts and numerous partners?
M/F/Both	Which gender's fantasies were more focused on "commitment and romance"?
M/F/Both	Who finds infidelity more hurtful?
M/F/Both	Who has a sex drive that is more consistent from week to week?
M/F/Both	Who is more interested in mating with someone older?
M/F/Both	Who is more interested in mating with someone younger?

If men and women are essentially the same, as some in our culture want to argue, this little quiz might be tricky for you. Actually, there is only one question where male and female are essentially the same.[12] The rest are exactly what you would think they are! And are so across cultures.

Is There a Male or Female Personality?

Do male and female demonstrate different personalities in how they live and view their lives and interact with others? If so, how distinct are these differences, and how reliable is the research?

The answers are absolutely, considerable, and quite!

Personality inventories collected from twenty-six different cultures indicate that the personalities of male and female are robustly gender distinct. The scholars conducting the study explain, "Gender differences are modest in magnitude" but "consistent with gender stereotypes, and replicable across cultures."[13]

Men rank substantially higher in assertiveness and women much higher in nurturance. Women are more likely to exhibit fearful emotions and anxious concern as well as wishes and encouragements to improve family situations and conditions. Men are typically more adventurous, excited, and willing to take risks and move out into new areas. They are also more overtly influential in terms of leadership. Women are consistently more affectionate and sentimental.

In addition, the personality inventories revealed that men work more in the mental arena of ideas and women more in the emotional arena of feelings and intuition. The literature affirms that one gender is more "emotional" while the other tends to be more "logical." Professor Alan Feingold, one of the early scholars to survey and summarize the growing body of research on gender personality differences across diverse cultures, explains that these differences have remained largely consistent both through generations and across nations. He adds that these findings indicate "a strong biological basis" for these gender-distinct personality traits.[14]

In addition, there are strong and consistent findings in vocational interests throughout the world: men are more likely to engage in investigative and building interests, while women rank higher in a variety of artistic and relational interests.

Another study took an interesting turn. In collecting data throughout fifty cultures on six continents, the researchers decided to go beyond what the data collectors found in their fieldwork to also examine how *male and female* data collectors themselves differed in their judgment and interpretation of findings from their subjects. Women, more so than men, were less critical of subjects and were more likely to describe them in positive ways, focusing and reporting more on positive personality qualities like gregariousness, warmth, trustworthiness, and altruism.[15]

Following is a quick rundown of additional miscellaneous male-female differences documented in the cross-cultural research literature:[16]

- Women tend to smile more often than men.
- Both men and women prefer to look at female bodies than male bodies.
- Women focus more on their appearance than men.
- Females make up more than 90 percent of all anorexia and bulimia sufferers.
- Men have stronger self-confidence about their appearance.
- Women tend to overestimate men's preference for slender females; men's ideal female body shape is heavier than what women assume it is.
- Males attempt suicide much more often than females.
- Males succeed at suicide more often than females.
- Male suicides are far more violent than females'.
- Boys have higher athletic confidence and self-esteem than girls.
- Females perform better academically and receive better grades than boys, but their academic self-esteem is similar.
- Men are more assertive, more inclined to take chances, and more open to ideas.
- Women are more tender-minded, agreeable, warm, and open to feelings.
- As children, girls play in smaller social groups that are more emotionally intimate.
- Adolescent girls are more expressive in their relationships than boys.
- Adult women report that their friendships involve greater communication and exchange of thoughts and feelings than men report of their friendships.
- Adolescent girls' relationships are more unstably dynamic, and they show greater retaliation when relationships end than boys do.

- Girls generally have higher behavioral and moral self-esteem than boys.
- Women tend to show higher levels of life satisfaction compared to men.
- Boys are more likely to express emotional problems externally by actions; girls are more likely to express their emotional problems internally.
- Women tend to be more trusting and more disappointed by broken promises than men tend to be.

Regarding gender distinction in personal self-esteem, the most significant differences included the following:

Greater self-esteem for men in:	*Greater self-esteem for women in:*
• physical appearance	• behavioral conduct
• athletic ability	• ethical considerations
• personal self-appraisal	• relational competence
• general self-satisfaction and self-esteem	• nurturance and care

Some of these measures—physical appearance and athletics for boys and ethical considerations for girls—were double for one gender than for the other across diverse cultures.[17]

WHEN GENDERS ARE FREE TO BE

Recent research into gender differences across various distinct cultures is surfacing interesting information that is counterintuitive to the twenty-first-century mind.

Given that cultures are different and that male and female differences are demonstrated to varying degrees in different cultures, where would you imagine gender differences between male and female to be most pronounced?

In traditional, developing cultures, where there is less freedom and where men and women have to depend on each other for daily survival, where each day's food is collected, prepared, cooked, and consumed immediately?

Or…

In modern cultures that are more technologically and economically advanced, where men and women have the resources and cultural freedoms to become and do what they desire?

It appears that when they enjoy greater freedom—both financially and culturally—men become more stereotypically masculine and women more stereotypical feminine. And this is most true for women. Personality tests were analyzed in more than sixty countries, and the *New York Times* summarizes the findings: "It looks as if personality differences between men and women are smaller in traditional cultures like India's or Zimbabwe's than in the Netherlands or the United States." The *Times* concludes, "The more Venus and Mars have equal rights and similar jobs, the more their personalities seem to diverge."[18]

This research was led by David P. Schmitt, director of the International Sexuality Description Project. He observed that, as wealthy modern nations remove the old barriers between men and women, it appears that "some ancient internal differences are being revived."[19] So, according to these findings, when men and women have the opportunity—provided by greater education, financial resources, and political and cultural freedom—to move beyond traditional gender expectations and roles to become whatever they want to be, they actually become even more distinctly masculine or feminine! The *New York Times* reported on this new research in 2008, but earlier research by various scholars in 2001 and as early as

1990 arrived at essentially the same conclusion: in more developed, individualistic, progressive, and egalitarian countries, gender differences don't shrink, but instead become conspicuously magnified.[20]

Professor Schmitt concludes, "An accumulating body of evidence, including the current data, provides reason to question social role explanations of gender and personality development."[21] When we are free to become what we want, we tend to become more gender distinct.

It's interesting to note how recent and increasingly robust and rigorous science disproves the claims of early gender theory. In the mid-1970s psychology professor Lois Hoffman wrote, "Adult sex roles are converging, and therefore sex differences among children and future generations of adults can be expected to diminish."[22] Contrast her statement with a 2001 finding from a major literature survey on sex typing (the way that gender difference is understood and exhibited) which found,

> Taken overall, a substantial body of research reveals a very clear picture: in spite of widespread expectations and desires, the various aspects of gender differentiation are not disappearing, if anything there is an *increase* in sex-typing, especially with the pattern most expected to decline, the femininity of females.[23] (emphasis added)

The authors of this study report they found no evidence whatsoever, in the twenty years leading up to their study, toward a more androgynous perception and demonstration of gender personality for either sex but rather a dramatic increase in gender distinction—and this is consistent with other studies on the subject.

A 2008 study across fifty-five different cultures states it more emphatically:

These findings strongly refute the social role model approach in which greater gender equality within a society should lead to smaller sex differences. In fact, the opposite has now been documented across multiple samples—increasing gender equality in a society results in larger sex differences in personality traits.[24]

The consistency of differences—and the kinds of differences—in males and females as evidenced in cross-cultural studies provides strong support for the idea that these "stereotypes" of male and female are more deeply rooted in biology and the nature of being male and female than in being culturally driven.

I think one of the primary reasons that males have become more masculine and females more feminine is in their sheer psychic and emotional comfort in being so. People in more prosperous countries are voting with their resources and freedoms and becoming more stereotypically gender distinct. Mate attraction also plays an important role. As finding a man or woman gets more difficult because of rising expectations, busy schedules, and lack of time to really get to know someone, both men and women are becoming more distinctly sex typed in order to attract prospective mates. Their advertising gets more vivid and focused, if you will.

SEX ON THE BRAIN

Finally, let's look at one of the most interesting and scientifically sophisticated areas of developing knowledge about how different the two parts of humanity are: brain research and neurobiology. A number of books, well researched and thorough, have been published in the past thirty years that explain intricate and profound sex distinctions in the seldom-seen places deep inside the human body.

One of the earliest popular books on this subject is *Brain Sex: The*

Real Difference Between Men and Women by Dr. Anne Moir and David Jessel. In the first line of their book, they explain that men and women are indeed different, equal only in their dual membership in humankind. The authors warn, "To maintain that they are the same in aptitude, skill or behaviour is to build a society based on a biological and scientific lie."[25] They further note,

> It is time to cease the vain contention that men and women are created the same. They were not, and no amount of idealism or Utopian fantasy can alter the fact. It can only strain the relationship between the sexes....
>
> The truth is that virtually every professional scientist and researcher into the subject has concluded that the brains of men and women are different. There has seldom been a greater divide between what intelligent, enlightened opinion presumes—that men and women have the same brain—and what science knows—that they do not.[26]

I like their informed frankness. As I hear their warning, I'm reminded that Satan—the enemy of God and our souls—first went to work setting Eve against Adam, and both of them against God. The Enemy is doing the same today with the lie that male and female are essentially not different, even though so much of our very being and experience (and deep and detailed research) tells us otherwise.

Other books like Deborah Blum's *Sex on the Brain: The Biological Differences Between Men and Women* (Penguin, 1997) and Doreen Kimura's *Sex and Cognition* (MIT Press, 2000) delve deeply into explaining what science is still discovering about brain, neural, and hormonal differences in the genders. Kimura opens her book with a quote by Kenneth H. W. Hilborn, professor emeritus at the University of Western Ontario: "When science ignores facts in favour of ideology...it ceases to be science and becomes propaganda for a dogma."[27] Perhaps the most significant recent contribution to this area of knowledge is in the work of Louann Brizendine, in particular *The Female Brain* and *The Male Brain,* which I've quoted from earlier in these pages.

What this growing body of research teaches us is that, in human experience and cultures, there truly is something distinct and important called womanhood. There is also something important and distinct called manhood. The two, as two halves of humanity, have much in common. But they also differ in important ways, which is the substance of this book. As the distinguished professor—and feminist scholar—Alice Rossi said in her presidential address at the annual meeting of the American Sociological Association in 1983, "Men bring their maleness to parenting, as women bring their femaleness."[28]

These distinctions have important implications and outcomes for our families, our children's development, and the safety, productivity, and strength of our communities. No society has ever figured out a way to raise healthy boys and girls into thriving men and women without mothers and fathers working together in this essential human task. And there are deep reasons for this, as I've detailed in these pages.

SEX OR GENDER? GENDER OR SEX?

Lastly, I want to address the use of the two words *gender* and *sex.* This issue is more of an ideological and political issue than a scientific one, but deserves quick attention. I am often challenged in this by gender studies professors and students who confuse the two.

I have used the two terms interchangeably on purpose. But many people in the "softer" sciences do not. For them, sex is about what you have between your legs; gender is about what you have between your ears. They explain that sex is more set, while gender is more fluid, in that it's whatever you perceive yourself to be.

However, if you follow this line of thinking, I can't understand why there are not seven billion different genders, because doesn't each of us perceive ourselves, even in our sex, a bit different from anyone else? I am a different kind of male than you are. She is a different kind of female than you are. It really gets kind of silly.

Curiously, if you're a student of the hard science of biology, no distinction is made between the terms *gender* and *sex*. The two words are synonymous, and thus they should be. Having worked in this field, published on it, and debated the issue of gender publicly at secular university campuses many times a year for the past eight years, I find the distinction some make here more sophistry than science. Yes, there are transgendered folks, people whose perception of themselves is at odds with their physical bodies. I've interviewed many of them. There are also intersexed persons, people born with ambiguous genitalia. The transgendered are much more politically active than the intersexed. The former are fighting for recognition of their nature as a natural and normal variation of human experience. The latter are simply trying to understand what their gender actually is without the guidance of typical physical characteristics.

The transgendered and intersexed are exceptionally rare human anomalies. Unfortunately, some babies are born without arms or with an extra arm. This doesn't mean they are a new, unheard-of kind of human being. It means their arms didn't develop normally. And we receive these people with their struggles, and love and care for them the best we can, working to help them live as normal a life as possible. But in all my speaking across the world, I have yet to meet one of these third, fourth, or fifth kinds of genders. All I ever find are variations on male or female.

An interesting academic article was published by a Harvard University biologist a few years ago on the different ways that biologists and psychologists and women's studies folks view the gender-sex question. This biologist studied the titles of academic articles published by people working in the natural sciences and the titles of articles published by those in the humanities and social sciences from 1945 to 2001, some thirty million article titles in all! He found that, prior to the early 1960s, the use of *gender* in titles was extremely rare in both the social and natural sciences. The first use of *gender* in this sense was in 1955 in an article by a Johns Hopkins sexologist, Dr. John Money, who laid the foundation for this theory that sex is physical and gender is psychological and the two do not necessarily correspond. But today Money's life work has been dramatically and utterly discredited by his own tragic and arrogant experimentations as well as in the hard sciences that we have reviewed here.[29] However, this hasn't deterred some from adopting *gender* in the place of *sex*. In the social sciences, arts, and humanities, *gender* is the preferred term, nearly to the exclusion of *sex*; in the hard sciences of biology and such, the use of *gender* is significantly less common.[30]

Professor J. Richard Udry, a leading sociologist from the University of North Carolina, Chapel Hill, opened his 1994 presidential address on the nature of gender to the distinguished Population Association of America by humorously welcoming all his "colleagues of the feminine gender, the masculine gender, and other genders not yet constructed." In this important address, he observed, "Today we use *gender* to indicate endorsement of a theory of gender as a human social invention."[31]

This theory has been proven untenable by an avalanche of increasingly sophisticated scientific discovery and careful human observation. That's why I use these two terms interchangeably. They are two words to refer to two things: male or female.

Notes

Introduction: The Importance of Difference

1. For a detailed explanation of my usage of the terms *gender* and *sex*, please see "Sex or Gender? Gender or Sex?" in the appendix of this book.

2. Leon R. Kass, *The Beginning of Wisdom: Reading Genesis* (New York: Free Press, 2003), 37.

3. Louann Brizendine, *The Female Brain* (New York: Broadway Books, 2006), 1.

Chapter 1: What Makes a Good Man?

1. Michael Gurian, *What Could He Be Thinking? How a Man's Mind Really Works* (New York: St. Martin's, 2003), 61.

2. Gurian, *What Could He Be Thinking?* 46.

3. Paul Okami and Todd K. Shackelford, "Human Sex Differences in Sexual Psychology and Behavior," *Annual Review of Sex Research* 12 (2001): 202.

4. Gurian, *What Could He Be Thinking?* 108.

5. Louann Brizendine, *The Female Brain* (New York: Broadway Books, 2006), 5.

6. Ronald Rohner and Robert Veneziano, "The Importance of Father Love: History and Contemporary Evidence," *Review of General Psychology* 5, no. 4 (December 2001): 382–405.

7. Margaret Mead, *Male and Female: A Study of the Sexes in a Changing World* (New York: William Morrow, 1968). Mead explains this in chapter 9.

Chapter 2: What Makes a Good Woman?

1. Michael Gurian, *What Could He Be Thinking? How a Man's Mind Really Works* (New York: St. Martin's, 2003), 46.

2. Simon Baron-Cohen, *The Essential Difference: Male and Female Brains and the Truth About Autism* (New York: Basic Books, 2003), 1.

3. Havelock Ellis, *Studies in the Psychology of Sex* (Philadelphia: F. A. Davis, 1910), 1.

4. Gurian, *What Could He Be Thinking?* 23.

5. Robert T. Michael and others, *Sex in America: A Definitive Survey* (Boston: Little, Brown, 1994), 124–29; Edward O. Laumann and others, *The Social Organization of Sexuality: Sexual Practices in the United States* (Chicago: University of Chicago Press, 1994), 364, table 10.5; Andrew Greeley, *Faithful Attraction: Discovering Intimacy, Love and Fidelity in American Marriage* (New York: Tom Doherty Association, 1991). The authors explain this in chapter 6.

6. Donna Freitas, *Sex and the Soul: Juggling Sexuality, Spirituality, Romance, and Religion on America's College Campuses* (New York: Oxford University Press, 2008), xv–xix.

Chapter 3: What a Boy Needs Most

1. Harvey C. Mansfield, *Manliness* (New Haven, CT: Yale University Press, 2006), 2.

2. Margaret Mead, *Male and Female: A Study of the Sexes in a Changing World* (New York: William Morrow, 1968), 103.

Chapter 4: What a Girl Needs Most

1. Steven Stack and J. Ross Eshleman, "Marital Status and Happiness: A 17-Nation Study," *Journal of Marriage and the Family* 60 (1998): 527–36; Glenn T. Stanton, *Why Marriage Matters: Reasons to Believe in*

Marriage in Postmodern Society (Colorado Springs: Piñon, 1997);
Debra Umberson, "Family Status and Health Behaviors: Social Con-
trol as a Dimension of Social Integration," *Journal of Health and Social
Behavior* 28, no. 3 (September 1987): 306–19; Debra Umberson,
"Gender, Marital Status and the Social Control of Health Behavior,"
Social Science Medicine 34, no. 8 (April 1992): 907–17; Debra Umber-
son and others, "The Effect of Social Relationships on Psychological
Well-Being: Are Men and Women Really So Different?" *American
Sociological Review* 61, no. 5 (October 1996): 837–57.

2. C. G. Jung, *Memories, Dreams, Reflections* (New York: Vintage, 1989),
   356.

3. Pamela Stone, *Opting Out? Why Women Really Quit Careers and Head
   Home* (Berkeley and Los Angeles: University of California Press,
   2007).

4. Stephanie Ventura, "Changing Patterns of Nonmarital Childbearing
   in the United States," *NCHS Data Brief,* no. 18, U.S. Department of
   Health and Human Services, May 2009, 2, fig. 2; 5, fig. 6; Lisa Mincieli and others, "The Relationship Context of Births Outside of Marriage: The Rise of Cohabitation," *Child Trends Research Brief,* May
   2007, 3, fig. 4; Daniel Lichter and Zhenchao Qian,
   "Serial Cohabitation and the Marital Life Course," *Journal of Marriage
   and Family* 70, no. 4 (November 2008): 861–78.

5. Wendy Shalit, *A Return to Modesty: Discovering the Lost Virtue* (New
   York: Touchstone, 1999), 67–69.

6. Louann Brizendine, *The Female Brain* (New York: Broadway Books,
   2006), 12.

7. Michael Gurian, *The Wonder of Girls: Understanding the Hidden Nature of Our Daughters* (New York: Pocket Books, 2002), 34.

8. Louann Brizendine, *The Male Brain* (New York: Broadway Books,
   2010), 12–15.

Chapter 5: The Journey to Manhood: Making Healthy Men out of Healthy Boys

1. Stephanie Ventura, "Changing Patterns of Nonmarital Childbearing in the United States," *NCHS Data Brief,* no. 18, U.S. Department of Health and Human Services, May 2009, 2, fig. 2; 5, fig. 6; Lisa Mincieli and others, "The Relationship Context of Births Outside of Marriage: The Rise of Cohabitation," *Child Trends Research Brief,* May 2007, 3, fig. 4; Daniel Lichter and Zhenchao Qian, "Serial Cohabitation and the Marital Life Course," *Journal of Marriage and Family* 70, no. 4 (November 2008): 861–78.

2. Margaret Mead, *Male and Female: A Study of the Sexes in a Changing World* (New York: William Morrow, 1968), 189.

3. Amy A. Kass and Leon R. Kass, eds., *Wing to Wing, Oar to Oar: Readings on Courting and Marrying* (Notre Dame, IN: University of Notre Dame Press, 2000), 1.

4. Arland Thornton and Linda Young-DeMarco, "Four Decades of Trends in Attitudes Toward Family Issues in the United States: The 1960s Through the 1990s," *Journal of Marriage and Family* 63, no. 4 (November 2001): 1009–37; Mindy E. Scott and others, "Young Adult Attitudes About Relationships and Marriage: Times May Have Changed, but Expectations Remain High," *Child Trends Research Brief,* July 2009, 5–6; Associated Press, "Youths' Stuff of Happiness May Surprise Parents," MSNBC.com, August 20, 2007, www.msnbc.msn.com/id/20322621; Colin Fernandez, "Forget Astronaut Dreams, Most Kids Just Want a Happy Marriage," *Daily Mail,* (UK), September 10, 2007.

5. Of course we'll never know the exact details of Ismay's behavior before the sinking of the ship, and perhaps history vilifies him to an extreme. However, according to recent revelations made by Louise Patten, a writer and granddaughter of *Titanic's* second officer Charles Lightoller, two mistakes sank the *Titanic:* a fatal steering error and a compound-

ing speed error. At the final meeting of the ship's officers, Lightoller "heard not only about the fatal mistake but also the fact that J. Bruce Ismay…persuaded the captain to continue sailing, sinking the ship hours faster than would otherwise have happened." Reuters, *"Titanic* Sunk by Steering Mistake, Author Says," September 22, 2010, www .reuters.com/article/idUSTRE68L1HG20100922.

6. *The State of Our Unions, Marriage in America 2009, Marriage and Money* (Charlottesville, VA: National Marriage Project and Institute for American Values, 2009), 68, www.virginia.edu/marriageproject/ pdfs/Union_11_25_09.pdf.

Chapter 6: Metamorphosis to Womanhood: Making Healthy Women out of Healthy Girls

1. George Gilder, *Men and Marriage* (Gretna, LA: Pelican, 1986), 18.

Chapter 7: Why It's Good When Mom and Dad Disagree

1. The only book I have found that addresses the topic in any way is my friend David Popenoe's excellent *Life Without Father* (New York: Free Press, 2006), where he gives it a chapter. But there is a wealth of data in hundreds of academic articles and books I have researched that together provide the tiles of the mosaic that is this book. It must be said, however, that it was Professor Popenoe's informative and illuminating chapter that sparked my interest in this topic many years ago and motivated me to expand on what he initially reported.

2. Henry B. Biller, *Fathers and Families: Paternal Factors in Child Development* (Westport, CT: Auburn House, 1993), 12.

3. Erich Fromm, *The Art of Loving* (New York: Harper and Row, 1956), 41.

4. Kyle D. Pruett, *Fatherneed: Why Father Care Is as Essential as Mother Care for Your Child* (New York: Free Press, 2000), 17–34.

5. K. Alison Clarke-Stewart, "And Daddy Makes Three: The Father's Impact on Mother and Young Child, *Child Development* 49, no. 2 (June 1978): 466–78; Kyle D. Pruett, "Role of the Father," *Pediatrics* 102, no. 5 (November 1998): 1253–61.

6. Pruett, "Role of the Father," 1255.

7. Pruett, "Role of the Father," 1255.

8. Ross D. Parke, *Fatherhood* (Cambridge, MA: Harvard University Press, 1996), 50–51.

9. Clarke-Stewart, "And Daddy Makes Three," 467.

Chapter 8: The Serious Business of Play

1. Donald E. Brown, *Human Universals* (Boston: McGraw-Hill, 1991), 59.

2. K. Alison Clarke-Stewart, "And Daddy Makes Three: The Father's Impact on Mother and Young Child," *Child Development* 49, no. 2 (June 1978): 466–78; Kyle D. Pruett, "Role of the Father," *Pediatrics* 102, no. 5 (November 1998): 1253–61.

3. Eleanor E. Maccoby, *The Two Sexes: Growing Up Apart, Coming Together* (Cambridge, MA: Harvard University Press, 1998), 266.

4. David Popenoe, *Life Without Father: Compelling New Evidence That Fatherhood and Marriage Are Indispensable for the Good of Children and Society* (New York: Free Press, 1996), 144.

5. Maccoby, *The Two Sexes*, 85–86.

Chapter 9: How Moms and Dads Together Influence Language Development

1. Henry B. Biller, *Fathers and Families: Paternal Factors in Child Development* (Westport, CT: Auburn House, 1993), 105.

2. Kyle D. Pruett, "Role of the Father," *Pediatrics* 102, no. 5 (November 1998): 1253–61.

3. Eleanor E. Maccoby, *The Two Sexes: Growing Up Apart, Coming Together* (Cambridge, MA: Harvard University Press, 1998), 269.

4. Elizabeth Bing, "The Effect of Childrearing Practices on the Development of Differential Cognitive Abilities," *Child Development* 34, no. 3 (September 1963): 631–48; Norma Radin, "Father-Child Interaction and the Intellectual Functioning of Four-Year-Old Boys," *Developmental Psychology* 6, no. 2 (March 1972): 353–61.

Chapter 10: Balancing Grace and Discipline

1. Carol Gilligan, *In a Different Voice: Psychological Theory and Women's Development* (Cambridge, MA: Harvard University Press, 1982).

2. David Popenoe, *Life Without Father: Compelling New Evidence That Fatherhood and Marriage Are Indispensable for the Good of Children and Society* (New York: Free Press, 1996), 145.

Chapter 11: Preparation Versus Protection: Why Both Dad and Mom Are Right

1. Karen Peterson, "Looking Straight at Gay Parents," *USA Today*, March 10, 2004, 2D.

Chapter 12: Your Child Is a Sexual Being

1. Donna Freitas, *Sex and the Soul: Juggling Sexuality, Spirituality, Romance, and Religion on America's College Campuses* (New York: Oxford University Press, 2008), xiv–xviii.

2. Joan R. Kahn and Kathryn A. London, "Premarital Sex and the Risk of Divorce," *Journal of Marriage and Family* 53, no. 4 (November 1991): 845–55; Jay Teachman, "Premarital Sex, Premarital Cohabitation, and the Risk of Subsequent Marital Dissolution Among Women," *Journal of Marriage and Family* 65, no. 2 (May 2003): 444–55.

3. Robert T. Michael and others, *Sex in America: A Definitive Survey* (Boston: Little, Brown, 1994), 131. Edward O. Laumann and others, *The Social Organization of Sexuality* (Chicago: University of Chicago Press, 1994).

4. Eleanor E. Maccoby, *The Two Sexes: Growing Up Apart, Coming Together* (Cambridge, MA: Harvard University Press, 1998), 142–43. Maccoby refers to thirty-nine separate studies showing this difference.

5. Suzanne G. Frayser, *Varieties of Sexual Experience: An Anthropological Perspective on Human Sexuality* (New Haven, CT: Human Relations Area File, 1985), 86.

6. Ronald Rohner and Robert Veneziano, "The Importance of Father Love: History and Contemporary Evidence," *Review of General Psychology* 5, no. 4 (December 2001): 382–405.

7. Jan Stets and Murray A. Strauss, "The Marriage License as a Hitting License: A Comparison of Assaults in Dating, Cohabiting, and Married Couples," *Journal of Family Violence* 4, no. 2 (June 1989): 161–80; Jan Stets, "Cohabiting and Marital Aggression: The Role of Social Isolation," *Journal of Marriage and Family* 53, no. 3 (August 1991): 669–80; Michael Gordon, "The Family Environment of Sexual Abuse: A Comparison of Natal and Stepfather Abuse," *Child Abuse and Neglect* 13, no. 1 (1985): 121–30.

8. Evelyn Bassoff, *Cherishing Our Daughters: How Parents Can Raise Girls to Become Strong and Loving Women* (New York: Dutton, 1998), 30.

9. Scott Coltrane, "Father-Child Relationships and the Status of Women: A Cross-Cultural Study," *American Journal of Sociology* 93, no. 5 (March 1988): 1060–1095.

10. C. S. Lewis, *Mere Christianity* (New York: Macmillan, 1960), 96.

11. Glenn T. Stanton, *My Crazy Imperfect Christian Family: Living Out Your Faith with Those Who Know You Best* (Colorado Springs: NavPress, 2004), 83–85.

12. Alan Booth and James M. Dabbs Jr., "Testosterone and Men's Marriages," *Social Forces* 72, no. 2 (December 1993): 463–77; Alan Booth and D. Wayne Osgood, "The Influence of Testosterone on Deviance in Adulthood: Assessing and Explaining the Relationship," *Criminology* 31, no. 1 (February 1993): 93–117; Alan Booth and others, "Testosterone, and Winning and Losing in Human Competition," *Hormones and Behavior* 23, no. 4 (December 1989): 556–71.

Chapter 13: How Mom and Dad Raise Kids Who Care

1. Richard Koestner, Carol Franz, and Joel Weinberger, "The Family Origins of Empathic Concern: A 26-Year Longitudinal Study," *Journal of Personality and Social Psychology* 58, no. 4 (April 1990): 713.

2. Cheri A. Vogel and others, "Relation Between Father Connectedness and Child Outcomes," *Parenting: Science and Practice* 6, nos. 2 and 3 (May 2006): 204.

3. John Snarey, *How Fathers Care for the Next Generation: A Four-Decade Study* (Cambridge, MA: Harvard University Press, 1993), 154.

4. Ross D. Parke and others, "Fathering and Children's Peer Relationships" in Michael E. Lamb, ed., *The Role of the Father in Child Development,* 4th ed. (Hoboken, NJ: Wiley, 2004), 315.

5. Henry B. Biller, *Fathers and Families: Paternal Factors in Child Development* (Westport, CT: Auburn House, 1993), 179.

6. David Popenoe, *Life Without Father: Compelling New Evidence That Fatherhood and Marriage Are Indispensable for the Good of Children and Society* (New York: Free Press, 1996), 148.

Appendix: Are Men and Women Really Different? Consulting the Sciences

1. Alice H. Eagly, "The Science and Politics of Comparing Women and Men," *American Psychologist* 50, no. 3 (March 1995): 155.

2. This is why Genesis 2:18 is perhaps the most profound statement about humanity in all of literature.

3. Wendy Wood and Alice H. Eagly, "A Cross-Cultural Analysis of the Behavior of Women and Men: Implications for the Origins of Sex Differences," *Psychological Bulletin* 128, no. 5 (2002): 705.

4. Wood and Eagly, "A Cross-Cultural Analysis," 718.

5. Todd Shackelford, David P. Schmitt, and David M. Buss, "Universal Dimensions of Human Mate Preferences," *Personality and Individual Differences* 39, no. 2 (July 2005): 456.

6. Kim Hill and A. Magdalena Hurtado, *Ache Life History: The Ecology and Demography of a Foraging People* (Hawthorne, NY: Aldine de Gruyter, 1996), 228.

7. Paul Okami and Todd K. Shackelford, "Human Sex Differences in Sexual Psychology and Behavior," *Annual Review of Sex Research* 12 (2001): 200.

8. David P. Schmitt, "Sociosexuality from Argentina to Zimbabwe: A 48-Nation Study of Sex, Culture, and Strategies of Human Mating," *Behavioral and Brain Sciences* 28, no. 2 (April 2005): 247–311.

9. David P. Schmitt (and 118 members of the International Sexuality Description Project), "Universal Sex Differences in the Desire for Sexual Variety: Tests from 52 Nations, 6 Continents, and 13 Islands," *Journal of Personality and Social Psychology* 85, no. 1 (July 2003): 85, 95.

10. Okami and Shackelford, "Human Sex Differences in Sexual Psychology and Behavior," 202.

11. Emily A. Stone, Aaron T. Goetz, and Todd K. Shackelford, "Sex Differences and Similarities in Preferred Mating Arrangements," *Sexualities, Evolution and Gender* 7, no. 3 (December 2005): 273.

12. Both men and women show the same levels of jealousy in response to a partner's infidelity but exhibit this in different ways and for different

situations. Women's anger and jealousy increases if the relationship is emotionally strong rather than merely physical. For men, there is no difference between emotional and nonemotional infidelity.

13. Paul Costa, Antonio Terracciano, and Robert R. McCrae, "Gender Differences in Personality Traits Across Cultures: Robust and Surprising Findings," *Journal of Personality and Social Psychology* 81, no. 2 (August 2001): 328.

14. Alan Feingold, "Gender Differences in Personality: A Meta-Analysis," *Psychological Bulletin* 116, no. 3 (November 1994): 429–30.

15. Robert McCrae, Antonio Terracciano, and 78 Members of the Personality Profiles of Culture Project, "Universal Features of Personality Traits from the Observer's Perspective: Data from 50 Cultures," *Journal of Personality and Social Psychology* 88, no. 3 (2005): 547–61.

16. Brittany Gentile and others, "Gender Differences in Domain-Specific Self-Esteem: A Meta-Analysis," *Review of General Psychology* 13, no. 1 (March 2009): 34–45.

17. Gentile and others, "Gender Differences in Domain-Specific Self-Esteem," 40–41.

18. John Tierney, "As Barriers Disappear, Some Gender Gaps Widen," *New York Times,* September 9, 2003, www.nytimes.com/2008/09/09/science/09tier.html.

19. Tierney, "As Barriers Disappear, Some Gender Gaps Widen."

20. John E. Williams and Deborah L. Best, *Sex and Psyche: Gender and Self Viewed Cross-Culturally* (Newbury Park, CA: Sage, 1990); Costa, Terracciano, and McCrae, "Gender Differences in Personality Traits Across Cultures," 329.

21. David P. Schmitt and others, "Why Can't a Man Be More Like a Woman? Sex Differences in Big Five Personality Traits Across 55 Cultures," *Journal of Personality and Social Psychology* 94, no. 1 (January 2008): 168–82.

22. Lois W. Hoffman, "Changes in Family Roles, Socialization, and Sex Differences," *American Psychologist* 32, no. 8 (August 1977): 646.

23. Lloyd B. Lueptow, Lori Garovich-Szabo, and Margaret B. Lueptow, "Social Change and the Persistence of Sex Typing: 1974–1997," *Social Forces* 80, no. 1 (September 2001): 16.

24. Schmitt and others, "Why Can't a Man Be More Like a Woman?" 176.

25. Anne Moir and David Jessel, *Brain Sex: The Real Difference Between Men and Women* (New York: Carol, 1991), 5.

26. Moir and Jessel, *Brain Sex,* 8, 9.

27. As quoted in Doreen Kimura, *Sex and Cognition* (Cambridge, MA: MIT Press, 2000), 1.

28. Alice S. Rossi, "Gender and Parenthood," *American Sociological Review* 49 (February 1984): 10. Rossi's article was the American Sociological Association 1983 Presidential Address delivered in Detroit, Michigan, in September 1983.

29. See John Colapinto's riveting and heartbreaking book on Money's incredibly arrogant and brilliant mistake: *As Nature Made Him: The Boy Who Was Raised as a Girl* (New York: Harper Collins, 2001). It is a must-read for those interested in the academic and political development of gender science.

30. David Haig, "The Inexorable Rise of Gender and the Decline of Sex: Social Change in Academic Titles, 1945–2001," *Archives of Sexual Behavior* 33, no. 2 (April 2004): 87–96.

31. J. Richard Udry, "The Nature of Gender," *Demography* 31, no. 4 (November 1994): 561.